ENGAGING
BENEDICT

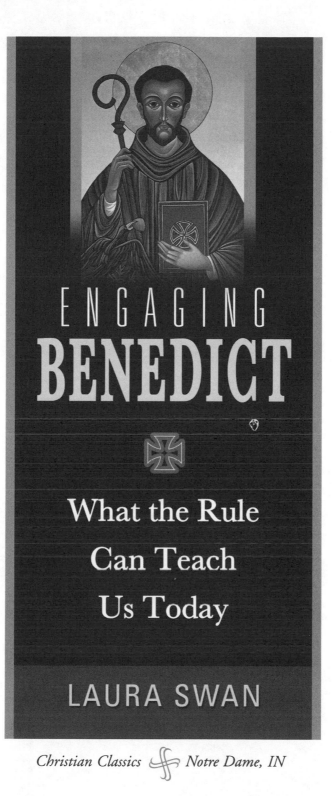

ENGAGING
BENEDICT

What the Rule
Can Teach
Us Today

LAURA SWAN

Christian Classics ❦ *Notre Dame, IN*

www.avemariapress.com

International Standard Book Number: 0-87061-232-8

Cover and text design by John Carson

Cover photo © Mary Charles McGough, O.S.B.; image courtesy of The Printery House, Conception Abbey, Conception, MO 64433

Printed and bound in the United States of America.

Library of Congress Cataloging-in-Publication Data

Swan, Laura, 1954-
  Engaging Benedict : what the rule can teach us today / Laura Swan.
     p. cm.
  Includes bibliographical references.
  ISBN 0-87061-232-8 (pbk.)
  1. Benedict, Saint, Abbot of Monte Cassino. Regula. 2. Spiritual life—Christianity.
I. Title.
  BX3004.Z5S93 2005
  255'.106—dc22
                              2004027145

Contents

Introduction

I began my Benedictine journey as an oblate. I was attracted to the beauty of praying the Liturgy of the Hours with its simple yet ethereal chant that encompassed the whole person. It was a natural fit for me that the search for truth in intellectual pursuits was also a significant piece of the search for God. I was drawn to the possibility of expressing one's spirituality through the creative arts; savoring the genius of artists, musicians, theater, and literature as an expression of passionate prayer has been essential to my spiritual journey.

I was attracted to the long history of powerful, creative, independent, and suffering women who consistently loved the Church into the future. Benedictine women thrived in the monasteries. I was equally attracted to a tradition that sought to live the Gospel ideal of women and men as full equals before Christ—through double monasteries. Benedictines are discerningly welcoming of many spiritual traditions without focusing on one alone. It is in listening to the many voices that the Voice of the One is beheld. The Benedictine way has been an inspiring and exhilarating path. I continue to enjoy the openness to creation as an expression of different aspects of the face of God.

When I entered the monastery in 1990, I had little perception of what I was getting into. I understood that I was entering an ancient tradition. I had some awareness that religious life as a whole had been undergoing changes but I didn't realize that *earthquake upon earthquake* was a more accurate statement of the reality. Benedictine women have been searching the origins of our tradition to resurrect the feminine face of monasticism and provide some guidance into the future. The challenge has been to find our call toward the prophetic edge of society and the Church.

I was plunged into a counter-cultural way of life that was being stretched by the realities of globalization. Monastic communities were springing up all over the world; increasingly these new communities were seeking to live the monastic way within their own indigenous culture. With increased contact and cross-fertilization, new possibilities and challenges were emerging. Monasteries have been meeting and networking, sharing resources and seeking to learn from one another. A sacred and stretching encounter for all. The gift of living with Benedictine women from East Africa as well as opportunities for travel have given me an appreciation for the nuances of Benedictine life found outside the dominant culture.

Encountering the Rule of Benedict during my initial formation years, I experienced life and possibility, challenge, dismay, and anger. While I was able to glean life-giving wisdom, I was consistently concerned with the voice and life experiences *not* found in Benedict's Rule and its interpretation. Writings that I encountered tended to presume a universal inclusivity of experience that was actually the experience of very few. Rarely were these writings critical of or questioning of Benedict's Rule. I found that I was constantly translating and reinterpreting sections of the Rule to fit my own self-understanding and life experience.

My monastic journey has been a total way of life that is focused on seeking God and therefore cannot be fragmented. We give our full humanity—mind, soul, body, emotions, desires, passions, and dreams—to God and the monastic community at our monastic profession. Aspects of our monastic profession include stability (meaning that I will seek God with this particular group of people), fidelity to the monastic way of life (I am committed to growth, learning, and transformation) and obedience (I commit to mutual discernment grounded in intense listening), chaste celibacy, and simplicity. Benedictines shy away from saying that we "take vows," rather we "make monastic profession." Our welcoming spirit, global awareness, and quiet pursuit of justice and reconciling relationships incarnates our monastic profession. This total way commits us to our radical journey.

Religious feminism is an interpretive tool that helps us discover ways that we may have inadvertently compromised the Good News. It is rather easy for humans to be seduced by the possibilities of power and greed. Religious feminism in its Christian context presumes that the Good News is for all and not a select few: based on gender, race, or access to power and economics. It presumes that liberation is a movement toward life; for Christians, this is Jesus who is *the Way, the Truth,* and *the Life.* Power is now empowerment: shared authority and mutual responsibility, nonviolence and collaborative leadership. Greed is transformed into *abundant simplicity* in lieu of a *scarcity mentality,* care for the environment, shared resources, and trust in a Providential God.

The Rule stands up to feminist critique, which is needed for a contemporary and passionate encounter with the monastic tradition. It is one way that monasticism will remain good news into the next century. With this same *listening with the ear of our hearts,* we are invited to engage Benedict's text with our contemporary challenges, pains, and aspirations. Standing in the monastic and desert traditions, Benedict beckons his followers to journey toward a deeper, more authentic, and vibrant relationship with God. Benedict's Rule was the "little way" for beginners.

A feminist analysis, when done within the context of religious faith, enriches us with the opportunity to envision new possibilities, make new connections, and invite us toward a richer, more diverse faith life. We are invited away from a dull, one-dimensional approach to Benedictine spirituality and the monastic way of life and into an exploration of a rich and ancient tradition.

Every generation and every culture must wrestle with Benedict's Rule, unpacking its meaning and wisdom for themselves. Each generation will have its problems with the Rule. To question and challenge the Rule is to bring empowerment to the seeker's spiritual journey. It is in wrestling with the Rule, and hence taking it seriously, that we find answers to difficult and painful questions. It is not disrespectful. Living texts run the danger of becoming a dying text if people do not engage them honestly. In very recent years, we are seeing the publication of new commentaries on the Rule of Benedict and Benedictine spirituality that take seriously the life experiences of women and people of diverse cultures. Hopefully this trend will continue.

With *Engaging Benedict,* I seek to explore problematic sections of the Rule or aspects of our way of life in light of recent work in the social sciences and women's experience. Contemporary concerns about globalization, cultural diversity, peace, and justice issues in the face of expanding militarism and materialism all find hope and direction in Benedict's Rule.

I do not propose that my thinking is a "definitive answer" for any or for all. I do hope that it models "permission" to realize that there are problematic texts that need to be wrestled with. Sacred texts engage every generation with prophetic challenges and compassionate encouragement. Living sacred texts challenge our comforts and fears, inviting us into possibilities and providing a framework for our creative chaos. Sacred texts, as living texts, speak to each generation. They are available to every culture and invite us to bring every aspect of our lives into our reading of them.

Throughout *Engaging Benedict* I often use my own translations of the Rule of Benedict, seeking inclusivity and ease of reading. I use "monastic" as the more inclusive term for the older "monk" and "nun." I use the contemporary "monastic leader" for the older "superior," "prioress," "abbess," "prior," and "abbot," each referring to the spiritual and temporal leader of the monastery. You may want to have your own copy of the Rule nearby to consult. *RB 1980* and *Benedict's Rule* (both cited in the Bibliography) are the two standard texts currently available. There are other translations as well.

Textual analyses of the Rule of Benedict come primarily from the fine work of Father Terrence Kardong, O.S.B.; Father Adalbert de Vögué, O.S.B.; Sister Aquinata Böckmann, O.S.B.; and Sister Mary Forman, O.S.B. Any errors or misunderstandings are mine alone.

I am increasingly aware that the spiritual journey and the monastic way of life consist of a healthy tension between the individual and communal search for God. Writing is much the same. My thinking has been enriched by conversations with others, daily life in my monastery, and the writings of many. *Engaging Benedict* is the product of this rich gift. *Engaging Benedict* has evolved over time with my many attempts to understand, reflect upon, and articulate monastic culture. This is a work-in-progress; the basic meaning of the monastic way of life.

My time spent studying and pondering and reflecting on the Rule of Benedict has been enriching and rewarding. In bringing my questions and anger and confusion to this text, I am more aware of the truth: that the Rule is a sacred and living text. I come away wondering if anyone can really make this claim without having experienced an honest anger with some of Benedict's statements. We honor the monastic texts by wrestling with them, questioning them, bringing present-day problems to them, and letting the texts unpack our blindness and deafness. To challenge and question the Rule empowers us to take ownership for this document, living it in the present and into the future; it is not an act of disrespect.

Engaging Benedict is not an exhaustive commentary on the Rule of Benedict. Rather I chose sections that stir anger, that we are in danger of ignoring rather than confronting, or that touch upon tender current issues. I intentionally sought some of the best writings in the social sciences, contemporary voices on the frontline of pastoral care, and present-day prophets to bring to Benedict's Rule.

Lectio divina, an ancient form of prayer associated with Benedictines, is the reflective, meditative reading of sacred texts. The intent is prayerful formation of heart and mind rather than gaining information. While the Bible is the most commonly used sacred text, spiritual writings and poetry are also helpful. I use the term "living lectio" to suggest that any of the "stuff" of life is useful for our prayer; encounters with others (or even ourselves), daily happenings, unsettling news, and troubling texts offer us rich opportunities to ponder the ways God may be speaking to us. Readers are invited to bring their lives to Benedict's Rule.

My intent is to engage readers in their own reflective process. I hope that I am contributing to a healthy, needed conversation and possibly evoking a necessary difficult conversation. If your thinking is stirred, stretched, challenged, and affirmed, then this has been worth my effort.

CHAPTER ONE

Benedict and the Monastic Tradition

The Abbey of Monte Cassino rests high on a precipice, on the edge of a mountain range in central Italy facing toward the sea.[1] To get there, the pilgrim must drive many miles of dizzying switchback up the precipitous incline until arriving at the gate to the monastery. The pilgrim then must walk up a fairly steep hill and through two archways. Continuing upward and through the arched stone tunnel until reaching the top where the sun bursts forth, the pilgrim is greeted by deep green grass and rosebushes.

In the center of this first of several gardens the pilgrim will encounter a statue of the *Dying Benedict*. The pilgrim is invited into a moment of "living lectio." Saint Benedict, who committed his entire life to a singular pursuit of God in prayer, stands with his arms uplifted in praise of the One Whom He Loves. But due to his infirmities, Benedict is no longer able to raise his arms in prayer without assistance. So on each side of Benedict stands a monk, holding up their venerable leader, enabling Benedict to continue this life in a stance of prayer until death beckons him toward his Beloved.

There is a strong connection between this sculpture of the *Dying Benedict* and the image of Moses painted in Sacred Scripture.[2] The Israelites, led by Joshua, were in battle with Amalek; Moses, Aaron and Hur were watching from the hilltop. Whenever Moses held up his hand, Israel prevailed; whenever Moses lowered his hand, Amalek prevailed. As Moses grew weary, Aaron and Hur each held up one of Moses' arms. Hence, Moses' arms are held up with assistance in order to assure the victory of the Israelites in battle.

The image of the monastic doing battle is strong in Benedict's writings. The valiant monastic is victorious in battle against the false self, sin, and the Evil One. Certainly the realities of living in community with imperfect people can become a battle toward compassion, grace, and even civility.

Benedict spent much of his life in support of young monastics in their early days of learning the monastic way, shaping their inner journey and communal life together. In response, these monastics willingly gave their very practical support so that their spiritual elder and mentor could die as he lived. With "living lectio," the seeker may reflect upon the powerful images of mutual support and encouragement, of journeying together toward the Holy One, and of a healthy giving of self to assist others and to receive needed support in return.

Benedict's genius was in recognizing the power of journeying together. There is power and empowerment, healing and strength in living together and recognizing our mutual interdependence. In his Rule, provision was made for the learned to teach the illiterate.[3] The poor and low caste taught the rich to be more truly human: Our worth is found in our being loved by God rather than in our social position or wealth. Rank in the monastery was set by date of entrance, and the only adjustments allowed were for holiness, not one's station in life.[4] Senior members of the monastery mentored the young, and particularly gifted monastics would be sent to comfort and guide the immature and struggling. Compassionate elders sent by Benedict indirectly challenged troublesome monastics; only when absolutely necessary would he confront them face to face.[5] Benedict removed as many class distinctions as was possible.

Benedict understood that the success of one was the success of all; the failures of even one monastic were the failures of all. The monastic journey was and is a journeying together. When we take commitment to our community seriously, whether this is a monastery, family and extended friends, or parish and faith community, we remain steadfast for the long haul. Benedict was teaching his followers the strength of mutual support, guidance, and encouragement.

Sister Aquinata Böckmann, a Missionary Benedictine of Tützing, tells a wonderful story about herself. Sister Aquinata entered a monastery in Bavaria, one with potato fields. Novices were responsible for weeding these fields and were usually joined by several of the older Sisters. Sister Aquinata and all the other Sisters began together at the beginning of their assigned rows. Soon Sister Aquinata realized that she was far behind the other Sisters. She would then put her nose to the grindstone and work hard at her weeding. Soon she would find herself catching up with the others. Then yet again she would find herself falling behind the others. And again she would work harder, trying to catch up.

This continued on for most of the morning. It was not until she was nearing the end of her row that she realized what was happening: the older Sisters, knowing her physical frailty, had placed themselves in the rows on either side of Sister Aquinata. When she was falling behind, they would discreetly reach over and weed some of her row. So Sister Aquinata would reach stretches of her row that needed little work, as her elders had already done it, and this would allow her to catch up with the others.

These older, wise, and compassionate Sisters, *senpectae* in Benedict's language, could have simply finished weeding their row and gone away to rest. Instead they sacrificed some of their leisure to help a fragile novice succeed. Today this same call to sacrifice for us may involve letting go of personal success or accomplishments, time for quiet or play, or even prayer. We are challenged to see the fragile ones in our midst as gift and not burden.

This, I believe, is what Benedict tried to teach with his *little rule for beginners*. In choosing to journey together and sacrifice the possibility of our own personal success, we are enriched and strengthened beyond measure. The community's success becomes our goal.

Benedict and Monasticism

As early monasticism developed, each small community developed an oral "rule" that defined their common life together.[6] Over time, these Rules began to influence one another and common themes emerged. These emerging common themes began to be written down and somewhat codified. These Rules were, and continue to be, living guides to the spiritual journey and to community living, rather than legal documents.

A Rule is a codified way of life that defines how a group of people living together to seek God and in service will live out their life. Generally a Rule is spiritual as well as organizational: how the community will pray together, methods for incorporating new members, governance, service, care of the frail, as well as the values and goals of seeking God. The Rules of the monastic tradition that pre-date Benedict and influenced Benedict in writing his own Rule include the Rule of the Master; Basil's Short and Long Rules; Pachomius, Shenoute, and Augustine; as well as the writings of John Cassian.

The genius of cenobitic monasticism is that all monastics serve under the Rule—shoulder to shoulder—and the Rule takes precedence over the teachings of the leader. Cenobitic monasticism has a strong sense of mutual obedience to the Rule and the living tradition of monasticism in balance to any one leader. In earlier monasticism, called eremitic, followers gathered around and related on a one-to-one basis with a charismatic leader. There was little sense of fellow monastics supporting and teaching each other.

Benedictine scholar Terrence Kardong tells us that there is no arbitrary order to the phrase: *under a rule and monastic leader.*[7] Cenobitic monastics, including the leader, live together under the Rule that forms the basis of the monastic way of life along with the living tradition of the monastery.

The collective experience of that monastic community, reflecting upon and living out the Rule, forms the living tradition of that monastery. The monastery's living tradition is so called for a reason. Each and every monastery interprets its Rule in light of the local culture, the needs of the region and the call of the People of God. The Rule and the living tradition of the monastery is continually interpreted by the *senpectae* and an experienced monastic leader.[8] While core expressions of Benedictine monasticism remain essentially unchanged, this living tradition might include particular ways we celebrate feasts, unique touches to our communal prayer or special remembrances in our *horarium*.[9]

The living tradition keeps the monastery alert, alive, and growing. The Rule challenges monastics to stay faithful to the monastic tradition and to reinterpret this living tradition, heeding its call into the future. The monastic way of life calls us to continually interpret the gospel in light of current and local needs and realities. This way of discernment challenges us to hear the leading of the Holy Spirit and to respond from a supportive and often prophetic stance.

Benedict established his monasteries for beginners to the monastic life. His Rule is a synthesis of the already-established Christian monastic traditions. As a pragmatist, Benedict was creating a simplified version of pre-existing monastic Rules for sixth-century men: men of diverse cultures and social and educational backgrounds. Many of the men who entered his monasteries were also new to Christianity: barely baptized and nominally catechized upon entrance. He therefore made provision for their catechesis and spiritual formation.

Benedict was seeking to help new monastics understand and appropriate the spiritual journey. Benedict believed that the most effective way to learn to be a monastic was to simply do monastic things. With practice, the young monastic's heart would begin to change, maturing in the monastic observance and in wisdom.

In writing his own Rule, Benedict synthesized the best of the many monastic Rules known in the Roman Empire. His Rule is a form of Wisdom Literature, a literary genre in which instructions for successful living are given and the perplexities of human existence are contemplated.[10] Wisdom Literature fosters an optimistic attitude toward the world; here in our ordinary life we can know God. God is ever-present and Holy Wisdom energizes, heals, and teaches those willing to be students of life. The Psalms, so central to Benedictine spirituality, are Wisdom Literature. Particular psalms are especially wisdom-oriented, emphasizing the harmony, order, and balance of creation and inviting humans to learn their right and humble place.[11]

Proverbs, Ecclesiastes, Job, and the Book of Wisdom are each examples of Wisdom Literature; there are strands of Wisdom Literature in the New Testament as well. The Sayings of the desert ascetics are also forms of Wisdom Literature.

Benedict's Rule is grounded in his life experience, his understanding of Gospel values, and prayerful reflection, all tested in the fires of persecution: very difficult monastics and monastic communities![12] Benedict's Rule makes significant use of scriptural references, including the Psalms, Proverbs, Sirach, and the wisdom-oriented Gospel of Matthew.[13] Each of these enriches his wisdom teachings.

Benedict established a *school for God's service* where his followers learned to be faithfully focused on the monastic and inner spiritual journey.[14] Benedict incorporates basic catechesis to the Christian life along with teachings on the monastic way.[15] The monastery was the place to learn the monastic way and to become like Christ to others.

Benedict intended his Rule to be flexible and adaptable to local prevailing conditions.[16] He gave his best advice on a specific situation, and then promptly invited his followers to adapt his guidelines to changing local needs. Today we see his Rule being adapted in many different cultures: common and familiar themes with the spice of the local culture and prevailing needs of the area blended in. Mixed communities—married, single, and vowed religious—are emerging; they share the Liturgy of the Hours and common ministries. They share the struggles and joys of the spiritual journey while living in different locations near their sacred space.

Oblates, or lay Benedictines, are on the increase around the world. Oblates live the Rule, interpreting it for their particular reality, and associate with the monastic community where they made their oblation. Oblates speak of the monastic values of balance, connection, prayer, and interior structure. As they deepen in their observance of the Rule, oblates notice that their lives have become more of an integrated whole. They find themselves more reflective and discerning in their work and political involvement. Oblates are publishing widely on the Rule, giving their keen insights into living this Rule in diverse situations and realities. Recently we have seen the Rule applied to families, using the wonderful and rich metaphor of the "family cloister."[17]

Businesses, including the health-care industry, have been looking to the monastic model for organization and ministry, even looking specifically at Benedict's Rule to find more effective and life-giving ways of being about their work. Some of the values they have discovered include Benedictine principles of discernment, organic and holistic organization, as well as balancing diverse talents among colleagues.

There are many examples seeded throughout Benedict's Rule where provision is made for adapting to prevailing needs. It is the spirit of the monastic rule that is to prevail. Benedict deeply respected the monastic tradition and the monastic rules that preceded him. However, he was not afraid to make adaptations to fit his own personal experience of what his followers needed. He intended that his followers have this same freedom to adapt according to local needs and particular situations.

In the midst of his careful and meticulous arrangement for praying the psalms at the *opus dei*, Benedict promptly gave permission for his other little monasteries to make adjustments if they had sufficient reason to do so.[18] Benedict was not rigid and legalistic. Praying the Divine Office was the priority for Benedict, not one particular way of doing so. Even as he provided freedom for local choice and adaptation, so Benedict was insistent that the heart of the monastic observance be protected and promoted.

In mundane and yet essential matters of food, drink, meal times, and clothing, Benedict made careful and thoughtful recommendations from the wisdom of his experience.[19] His recommendations were practical—allowing for diverse personalities, wants, and needs. Then he gave permission for changes to be made as local need dictates.

Benedict lived in an era when distinctly religious attire had already emerged. Monastic garb was simple, cheap fabric loosely cut; a work apron was available for farm and domestic work. Hair was cropped short and some women wore a simple head covering. The distinctiveness was in the rough simplicity of the garb, which was the attire of the very poor and slaves. Unfortunately some people were growing impressed with the meaning and advantages of this distinctly religious attire. They were wearing it with pride, and too often their lifestyle did not measure up to the meaning of the religious garb.

Benedict reclaimed monasticism as a lay religious movement and not a clerical one. He rejected monastic garb as a symbol of uniqueness and entitlement. Instead, he returned it to its proper place: simple, practical, and adaptable to local needs. Monastics were to wear better clothing while out on business and wear their work clothes at home in the monastery. Benedict's followers were making a point of not standing out in their religiousness by following the examples of other alleged "religious."

Monastic Culture

Monasticism, as an all-encompassing way of life, has an ancient culture. Monastic culture defines who we are and how we are in our world. Monastic culture encompasses the ideas, beliefs, values, activities, and knowledge of nearly two millennia of lived experience received. With entrance into the monastery, the new member is immersed into the culture. When monastics gather, there is a familiarity, a level of comfort or at-home-ness, despite some religious differences.

Monastic culture has always been an evolutionary process. The ways people live, pray, play, work, and minister together continue to grow. The manner in which members of a community communicate with one another and encourage and admonish one another has developed over time and continues to influence the development of monastic culture. Living life in deep and prayerful reflection and discernment shapes monastic life in the present and into the future.

Monastic culture is a complex and diverse communication system that influences and supports particular attitudes, behaviors, and outlooks on life, while defining the acceptable range of behaviors. Each monastery has its own spoken and unspoken set of norms that defines its communal life and culture. This includes knowledge of our monastic history, values, and traditions. Monastic Christians have reflected together upon our common belief in Jesus Christ with all its implications. Artistic and musical expressions evolve that are grounded in and expressive of our Christian faith and monastic way of life. Monastics have cultivated a particular outlook on life.

Monastic culture is expressed through the way we work with moral and ethical teachings, canon law and common customs, and those traditions that intersect with our inherited monastic tradition, local culture, and Christian faith. Monastic culture defines and guides the ways we interact with and prophetically challenge our regional culture.

Culture is a communal affair; one cannot be a culture alone. Culture is a group process and way of being together. Monastic culture is a dynamic process that is learned: at the affective (feeling, intuitive, bodily) level, cognitive (thinking, rational) level and symbolic level. We intuitively share common ways of how we perceive and know reality. Theologian Shawn Copeland tells us that culture is not merely:

> extrinsic, material, and static, but as dynamic, spiritual, and in-process. Moreover, this proposal adverts explicitly to human persons whose inquiry, understanding, persistence, and imagination are responsible for creating, sustaining, and transforming culture. For as culture realizes in the concrete the meanings and values that mold personal and interpersonal, religious and moral, economic and political choice, *imagination* has a crucial role.[20]

The work of an active imagination in culture-making is what keeps monasticism alive and vibrant. Every generation must wrestle with the implications of the received monastic tradition in light of the needs of the local People of God, the signs of the times, and the discerned call of the Holy Spirit. We absorb the tradition and the teachings of the *senpectae*, both living and deceased. Then we must begin to make sense of it all for our own lives and for the upcoming generation. We must wrestle with the question: *So what?* We must live with the possibilities as well as the call to be a prophetic challenge in the world and to each other. We must also be open to the prophetic challenges that all People of God are to us as monastics and seekers. How do we engage our imaginations in our monastic life? How do we intentionally listen to the cries and opportunities and possibilities around us—to shape new expressions of monasticism?

New forms of Benedictine monasticism are positively effecting monastic culture as a whole. The wisdom and lived experience of the laity is also having its influence on monastic culture. This engagement by each generation of monastics moves monastic culture into the future and is the very "stuff" of traditioning.

Monastic Traditioning

Traditioning is how we receive, internalize, and pass on the traditions of our culture within our families, monasteries, and other intentional communities. Traditioning is taught by immersion; it happens at the heart-belly, subconscious and unconscious levels of our being. Tradition holds the experiences of a people, including implicit and explicit understandings, myths, and stories. Tradition helps to actualize the potential of the human person. Tradition deeply impacts how we respond to life. We bring to reality our received feelings, memories, images, ideas, and attitudes. Tradition is both remembering and remembrance.

Theologian Jeanette Rodriguez speaks of "cultural memory" as the repository of the unique oral, intuitive, and written life of a people.[21] It includes voices raised in celebration and the tradition of a sacred place. Intergenerationally, some of these cultural memories are passed on intentionally, but much is passed on unconsciously and received by younger members. Cultural memory keeps a people "alive" in the matter of heart, soul, and intellectual identity. Cultural memory is especially important in times of upheaval, oppression, war, and brutal colonization. Cultural memory for monastics is the living traditions of 1800 years of Christian monasticism, particularly expressed in the Rule of Benedict. A particularly Benedictine cultural memory has kept the tradition alive, even strengthened that memory, through centuries of political upheaval, suppression, and evangelization among new peoples.

I have often pondered those people who have come to monasteries for the first time and experience an at-home-ness and comfort never found elsewhere. They speak of their oblation or monastic profession as an acknowledgment and celebration of a part of themselves unknown and unseen until they encountered the monastery. In discernment with a possible new member, we often look for evidence of a "monastic heart." Is this a type of cultural memory?

Monastic traditioning happens in many, diverse ways. For Benedictines, liturgy is very powerful. The ways we create and celebrate our public prayer and Liturgy of the Hours; our common ways of private prayer; contemplative prayer and lectio.[22] Liturgy includes the reenactment of our sacred texts, sacramental, and sacred events. Liturgy gathers together the experiences of being human in community to ritualize meaning, paradox, pain, and joy. Liturgy "stretches our imagination, to test the limits, to call us to larger and more inclusive ideas and views—all while preserving the fullness of the Christian experience."[23] The Liturgy of the Hours is the prayer of the Universal Church for the People of God; it is neither our private prayer nor even the prayer for the monastic community alone. Our experience of liturgy feeds and empowers our further integration into the sacred tradition of our communities.

Storytelling is another powerful tool for traditioning. Our stories feed the soul and imagination. Stories convey the vision and passion of our search for the Holy One that supports and moves us into the future, in ways far more complex and deep than intellectual information alone. Liturgy is storytelling: A retelling of sacred story. Storytelling encompasses the study of our monastic heritage and our lectio with monastic texts.

Observances form an affective and intuitive part of our storytelling. The fruit of our prayerful reflection, such as statio, days of quiet reflection, holiday celebrations, and moments of shared solitude and silence enrich our storytelling. These observances push the self-imposed boundaries of our thinking and presumptions, moving us beyond our world of comfort and fear. It is here that we encounter possibilities and our hopes are given impetus.

Traditioning occurs—powerfully—through our creative endeavors. Writing icons, carving, creating sculptures, painting, creation and performance of musical scores, research, and writing are but a few ways that monastics have traditioned the common life, spirituality, hopes, passions, and dreams. Symbols embody significant, deep experiences: the paschal mystery, a profound encounter with the Holy Other or the monastic tradition. Symbols such as the Sacred Heart, the Benedictine cross, a candle, or an icon express powerful concepts and memories far beyond the image itself.

The rituals that commemorate and celebrate the events of our lives—births and marriages, moving through the stages of incorporation into the monastery, grieving losses and celebrating special moments—all serve to continue the story and offer opportunities to retell the story with new insights and meaning.[24] Individual rituals weave our story and unique accent into the greater story of our community. Times and seasons of shared silence and solitude connect us heart to heart. Faith sharing, as we seek together to understand God's movement in our lives, to find the meaning of significant events, and to appreciate God's provident gifts to us create the heart of traditioning.

Traditioning occurs through our times of discernment. Sitting together—listening for the voice of the Holy One and sharing our sense of how God is moving and calling us forth—builds the intuitive "stuff" of monastic traditioning. When we seek to understand God's call in our life and decide how to live out this call we move forward in the tradition.

Traditioning happens whether we intend it or not. Looking at the living history of our families we wonder: Are we intentionally creating positive and evocative traditions with family gatherings, significant moments in our lives, and significant passings? Are our faith groups incorporating traditions that support our faith journey and values? Are we as oblates and monastics cultivating intentional traditions that mark who we are and how we want to be to the world?

The Living Tradition

The teachings of Benedict and the example of fifteen centuries of monastics wrestling daily with his Rule are finding new and creative expressions. The Holy Spirit is *thinking outside the box!* We are challenged to find fresh approaches and understandings.

Benedict wrote his Rule for men. There is no evidence that he had anyone in mind other than the men within his own monastery as well as the other monasteries he had established and left to the leadership of others. He was writing from his own Roman worldview and masculine life experience. Benedict simply was not writing his Rule with women, non-Romans, or contemporaries in mind.[25]

As a living text, Benedict's Rule has taken on a life of its own. A tradition of interpretation has developed over the centuries where one interested may study either the Rule itself, the context within which Benedict created his Rule, or the tradition of interpretation around this Rule.

Today we may approach the Rule with questions about justice, the institutional church, ecumenism, or globalization. Do we as monastics belong in the heart of our religious institutions, out on the prophetic edge, or somewhere totally new? How can the monastic way effectively embrace our diverse faith traditions without watering them down? What are the essentials of the monastic life that inform all expressions of Christianity?

Some monastics are now bringing the concerns of religious feminism to this text. Does Benedict's Rule affirm and support women and the marginalized, or does it perpetuate a patriarchy that diminishes all? How might the Rule guide and empower a movement through feminist, justice, and liberation concerns to something new that is truly collaborative and affirming for women and men? How does our monastic life encourage and support the necessary healing conversations that will push our faith traditions to truly and authentically proclaim the *good news* of Jesus rather than the *mediocre news*?

Are we growing into loving people? Do we allow the monastic way and Benedict's Rule to challenge us and shape us? Or have we tamed, homogenized, and pasteurized the Rule so that it no longer pierces our hearts into compassion? And isn't that the point of the monastic journey: To learn to love? To love one another into becoming loving people?

Chapter Two

Benedict's Good Monastic

The *Life of Saint Benedict* by Gregory the Great reveals a mature monastic whose life experience was rough and raw and real. Throughout Benedict's pursuit of the solitary and later monastic life, he encountered problems heaped on troubles. Fragile, loving people, ornery souls, and outright wicked monastics seasoned Benedict into a wise and discerning person. The reader might wonder if these early monastic communities did anything to screen entrants. Benedict's Rule reveals what he learned from hard, painful experience.

Benedict began his monastic life in an age when laxity and permissiveness was seeping into some communities, causing deterioration in observance and simple quality of life. Benedict encountered such communities and found them nearly impossible to reform. While the Rule of Benedict made provision for diverse personalities and needs, Benedict consistently warned monastics to be aware of the ways an insidious spirit of compromise could seep in. Benedict wanted to make monasticism accessible to the simple beginner, including the new convert, without compromising the tradition.

After beginning his Rule with a beautifully stirring prologue, Benedict then suddenly moved into a brief discourse on the "Four Kinds of Monastics."[1] Benedict was laying the foundation for his understanding of the two healthy and clearly preferred forms of monastic life: cenobitism and anchoritism.

Kinds of Monastics

✠

It is clear that there are four kinds of monastics. The first are the cenobites, who live in monasteries and serve under a rule and monastic leader (RB 1:1–2).

Living in community can take many different forms. Benedict was referring to the emerging form of monasticism that placed members in a lifelong committed relationship with one another, seeking God together while holding all things in common.

Community may be our committed faith community, family, or that group of people to whom we have a reciprocal covenant to encourage and support one another in our faith journey and ministry. It is made up of people who call us toward a deeper sense of self so that our journey toward selflessness is healthy and efficacious. Healthy community entices, supports, and challenges us toward the interior discipline and freedom that God desires for us. Communal living, in whatever form we are able to live, becomes the context for seeking and serving God and the people of God.

Community, family, colleagues at work, and our neighbors provide us with endless lessons on the spiritual life. They rub the rough edges of our personalities, expose our unhealthy attachments, and help us better understand our core values and life goals. Community challenges us to grow: to counteract our self-centeredness with an awareness of others and to attend legitimately to our inner world when the temptation is to give ourselves away.

Significant people in our life help guide us in our search for God. We are challenged to attend the call and demand that is within ourselves. We are also significant participants in the communal search for God. As interdependent beings, we are created to give support and encouragement to others as well as to receive. We are drawn out of ourselves and yet journey deep within in the very process of supporting others.

Community in all its varied forms calls forth from us our most essential, truest self. Community life effectively demands that we send away all the illusions and deceptions we developed in order to protect ourselves from pain. Community teaches us to discipline our lives and prioritize our limited time and resources. Community also affirms our worth, goodness, and gifts; oftentimes it draws from us what we never realized we possessed.

It is in the relationships that form our monastic journey that we learn the skills that lead to the fullness of maturity. Benedict tells us that *the workshop where we should work hard at all these things is the monastic enclosure and stability in the community.*[2]

Benedict says that *monastics should bear each other's weaknesses of both body and character with the utmost patience.*[3] Rather than looking for artificially imposed ascetical practices and then feeling guilty when we do not follow through, we ought to pay attention to the call God has already placed in our lives. Our asceticism is to treat our family, friends, colleagues, and community with profound respect, showing compassion and mercy at every available opportunity. We must be present to the present moment and embrace life with a stance of openness to all the ways God would lead us and teach us. We must receive constructive criticism and take it to prayer and equally to name criticism that is someone else's projection is ascetical.

"Living lectio" entices us to reflect on the ways that we are connecting with self, others, and God. How do we cultivate a healthy interdependence? Are we open, in a stance of vulnerability, to being supported and challenged by others? How do we actively support and encourage and challenge others in our life?

What Rule of life are we actively following? In what ways do we allow it to shape our commitments and choices? In what ways are we recognizing and responding to the asceticism life is handing us in this moment?

✠

> The second kind of monastics are the anchorites, or hermits. Their observance is no mere novice fervor, but the result of long testing in a monastery. Community support has taught them how to battle the evil one and this excellent training in the communal battle-line enables them to venture out to the single combat of the desert. There they are able to fight with God's help against vices of flesh and thought, relying on their own hand and arm rather than relying on the help of others (RB 1:3–5).

Benedict, like most of his day, believed that the true anchorite or hermit was the highest form of monastic and religious life. Yet he realized that the most effective place for those who yearned for a deeply intense relationship with God—the goal of the true anchorite—was in community. Here was the place of training, conversion, and transformation that prepared and equipped the person who desired a solitary life. To sidestep this important training too often led to a dissolute and wasted life.

The desert ascetics were clear that their life was singly focused on continual awareness of the presence of God. Their goal was to become one with the angels, to cultivate such an intense life of prayer that they literally became fire.[4] The lives of the desert ascetics were highly disciplined with prayer, study, hospitality, and work. Desert ascetics always made sure that they had alms to give to the poor. Their lives were other-oriented, not self-oriented. A true hermit was not in the desert to escape life.

Benedict and his colleagues believed that this single combat was the greatest challenge and achievement that the Christian could embrace. Yet he then dedicates the remainder of his Rule to cultivating cenobitic community life. Benedict seems to recognize this paradox without resolving it: if we learn the tools of the monastic spiritual life then we are well equipped for the desert, anchorite life and yet the cenobitic life is the most vigorous.

We all have a monastic and solitary within us. This is that part of ourselves that needs some rich, creative, and nurturing time alone. This is the place where we enter into contemplative prayer and/or go away for a few days or even weeks of solitude.

There are people in our midst that need a season of intense solitude, lasting several years. And we have those who have a clear calling to solitude as a way of life. Those who have been making the solitary journey for some time usually mentor our present-day solitaries. Rarely do we intuitively know how to effectively live this intense life of solitude. Without training, we could do serious psychological harm.[5]

"Living lectio" entices us to reflect on the ways that we allow the "hermit within" necessary time and attention. Do we carve out time for solitude and silence? Do we go away to be alone? Do we support those we are in committed relationship with, including our children, to take this time of solitude? In what ways has our God-centered time of solitude enriched our relationships and community life? What do we encounter in the depths of our silence? How do we recognize the differences between the solitude of a hermit and the isolation that breeds addiction and severs us from others?

✠

The third type of monastic is the Sarabaites, and they are wretched. They have been tested by no rule based on the criterion of experience. Unlike gold tested in the furnace, they are as soft as lead. They lie outwardly to God by their tonsure but still remain faithful to the world by their deeds. They live in twos and threes, or even alone, without a shepherd and in their own sheepfolds, not those of God. The craving of their appetites is the law for them. Their own opinions and desires they call holy; what displeases them they say is not permissible (RB 1:6–9).

The term "sarabaite," from the Copt for "separated from monasteries," was not originally a derogatory term; that evolved later. Benedict was aware that there was an increasing problem with self-defined monastics. These monastics wore the garb of religious life but were becoming a scandal to the Church and the monastic world.

Benedict condemned those who would claim to be monastic but whose behavior betrayed otherwise. Sarabaites were those who claimed to be monastic, yet rejected all authority but their own. Benedict called the monastic to be *under a rule and leader*. However, self-guided Sarabaites did whatever they wanted, when they wanted, and in whatever way they chose. They allowed no one to have command of their heart; they made their own decisions as they saw fit.

Sarabaites were self-willed, self-pleasing, fiercely independent, and opinionated. They defined monastic observance according to their present pleasure and goals. They stayed with those who cooperated with their self-centered ways, disappearing at the first sign of a challenge.

The Sarabaites undermined much that Benedict valued most. Where Benedict understood that commitment to place and people taught us much about the ways of God, the Sarabaites rejected remaining in one place and with one people. Sarabaites were constantly on the move, seeking the new experience and avoiding hard work and pain.

"Living lectio" faces us directly with the reality that we too are the Sarabaites. What helps us to recognize the Sarabaite within? What support and guidance do we need to let go of the false self (the Sarabaite) and embrace our true self (the cenobite or anchorite)?

We can be drifters, always on the move. We can seek endless distractions, without even leaving home. How are we growing aware of our internal warning signals when we are drifting again? How are we listening to this restless inner self in order to understand what we are avoiding or what authentic need we are failing to meet?

What acts as a counterbalance to our tendencies toward being opinionated, self-willed and always craving something? In what ways do we honor the internal warning signals that we are not receiving input and helpful criticism from those who are part of our inner circle of committed friends and community? Do we stay in relationship with those who honor us yet may disagree or challenge us, or do we seek new friends and a new community each time life gets uncomfortable?

Do we recognize the voice of sanity and balance in the midst of our driven society? With our fiercely independent culture, how do we heal our resistance to commitment and interdependence? Our monastic promise and oblation of stability, obedience, and conversion of life gives us tools to confront the Sarabaite within.

✠

> The fourth kind of monastic are called gyrovagues. They spend their whole lives wandering through various provinces, staying in the cells of different monastics for three or four days at a time. They are ever on the move and never stable. Slaves to their own wills and the delights of the palate, they are in every respect worse than the Sarabaites (RB 1:10–11).

Constant wanderers, gyrovagues moved from place to place, never in committed relationships. Commitments and relationships were easily broken. The horizon ever lured them to depart for something new and different. These were the false hermits. The ground constantly shifted around them and one never knew where they stood with them. They did not follow through on commitments, if ever they make a commitment to begin with. An inner storm and turmoil kept others and all of life at arm's length. Gyrovagues withdrew from responsibility while putting on a good face. It was all image and little depth or reality.

Gyrovagues were addicted to new experiences and the new thrill. They were chronically immature. Their monastic promise was made of words only; their life was one of escape from reflecting on the meaning of the words. There was little capacity for inner reflection, so their words and actions held little meaning for them. Distractions were urgent in order to stay perpetually on the move and never be pinned down. These were drifters in the fullest sense. Even if they were not physically on the move, their inner world was on the move: from idea to idea, from possibility to possibility.

"Living lectio" challenges us to care for the drifter within. Our hearts and minds wander; we are attracted to distractions. We are paralyzed by perfectionism, lured by hyper-responsibility or take great pains to avoid any responsibility. We contend with a restless spirit. What keeps us grounded, rooted, and connected to our community, family and friends? Are we committed to building and sustaining intimate friendships? Are there some people in our lives with whom we bare aspects of our soul, our struggles, and our hopes?

How do we balance care of self and care of others? How do we celebrate life's significant moments, friendships, and community without becoming enslaved to pleasure? Have we grown too comfortable with our internal warning signals?

Benedict's Good Monastic

✠

> It is better to be silent than to speak of the wretched lifestyle of these monastics. So putting these aside, let us with God's help turn to arranging a way of life for that most vigorous race, the cenobites (RB 1:12–13).

Benedict teaches that the most vigorous and challenging form of monasticism is living closely together in community like the cenobites.[6] Healthy cenobitic monasticism is dynamic. Every member takes responsibility to the best of their own ability to build positive, caring relationships. Monastics are mutually supportive. Each cares for the spiritual health of other members so that prayer, silence, and solitude are supported. Members challenge one another and are open to receiving guidance from one another.

Benedict's good monastic values the greater good of the community: actively seeking to build and protect the members as well as the community as a whole. The health and well-being of each individual member strengthens the whole. It takes healthy members to make a healthy monastic community. There is always a delicate balance between personal needs and the needs of community that creates and perpetuates a healthy, forward-moving atmosphere.

Benedict's good monastic deepens in awareness of those sources of stress, roots of conflict, and distortions of power that can harm and even destroy community relationships. Competitiveness, tendencies to undermine appropriate authority, and the need to control others or situations are usually an indicator of low self-esteem, self-will and fear. They can paralyze communities, disable communication, and divert attention and energies from the monastic observance. A monastic heart seeks to hone skills that enable and empower community. A monastic heart recognizes the Holy in others: in guests, the unwanted, and especially the poor; in the possessions of the community or family; and in the monastic space.[7]

Benedict's good monastic yearns to develop the fine skills of building loving, trusting, and enriching relationships, especially with those people we are not naturally attracted to. The cenobite does not need to argue, but trusts the process of community living and especially community discernment.[8] With open and honest relationships there is no room for gossip, grumbling, and the forming of "political camps."

Benedict's good monastic is a deep listener.[9] This kind of listening encompasses the fullness of our being. True listening involves an active response. It is a listening into being. Deep listening is fed and supported by the cultivation of quality silence. The monastic heart grows in its comfort with the silent place where storms and confusion and polarizing voices can be stilled and quieted.[10] Silence supports our growth in self-awareness, discernment, and simple confidence in ourselves. We come to know ourselves primarily in our silence and solitude. The monastic heart makes careful use of words: words can give life or destroy it through our anger, jealousy, or vindictiveness. Words are used carefully in support of the relationship.

Benedict looked for an immediacy of response from the individual heart that is in tune with the beating heart of the community. Benedict resisted the human tendency to dawdle and procrastinate that disrupts the rhythm of the community. Perpetual tardiness reveals lack of commitment or distraction; Benedict encouraged promptness of response.[11] For Benedict, to listen means to respond promptly.

Simple times of human activity, like meals and communal prayer, are crucial to building and sustaining healthy community. The good monastic is fully present at meals: showing up before the meal begins, honoring the silence during readings, serving quietly and efficiently—all of which makes the meal a positive and pleasant experience.[12] Yet community makes every effort to include the latecomers to assure their place at meals and prayers. Kardong points out that, for Benedict, meals are a primary symbol of community.[13] The Opus Dei and meals are pivotal points in the daily monastic schedule and can easily become points of contention when not properly honored.[14]

The good monastic takes care and concern for the quality of the Divine Office:[15] aiming to arrive early, in order to prepare for entering fully into the prayer of the Office as well as avoiding disruption by arriving late. Care is taken to chant the psalms properly in harmony and rhythm with the full community. The chapel is a place of reverence and silence, attitudes that are intentionally cultivated by all who enter. A monastic heart prefers nothing to the Opus Dei.

The good monastic's prayer is passionate and sincere, simple and to the point.[16] Prayer is not merely one more thing squeezed into an already overburdened schedule: One does not connect with the Divine and then resume tackling responsibilities. The monastic heart is immersed in prayer as a total way of life.[17] Gentle, compassionate prayer cultivates and sustains a yearning for prayer.

There is evidence when a person is maturing into the wise monastic Benedict desired each of his followers to become. Inner and outer worlds are congruent. The monastic heart is of *good repute and holy life,* known for *virtuous living and wise teaching,* seen as a *wise person, of mature character, and well-disciplined . . . not gluttonous, arrogant, violent, unfair, stingy, or wasteful.*[18] A mature monastic heart has a healthy sense of self, and is not strong-willed, stubborn or argumentative.[19] She grows in generosity and compassion, while being self-disciplined.[20] He is known for sympathy, tenderness, strength, and courage.[21]

The good monastic is open and willing to *serve one another;* she is able to give support as well as receive it.[22] He will *lavish great care on the sick, the children, the guests, and the poor,* expressing a tender compassion for the sick and frail.[23] She bears the *burden of one another,* creatively and with tenacious strength.[24] In cultivating these virtues, the good monastic deepens in a healthy sense of self.

The monastic heart is growing into one of Benedict's *senpectae,* a wise and compassionate elder; inspiring trust and confidence from other seekers who are then willing to listen and accept guidance. She is gentle in giving correction and exemplifies a contemplative stance.[25]

Benedict's good monastic is deepening in wisdom through the grace of the Holy Spirit, zeal for the monastic way of life and openness to learn from all of life.[26] He seeks help from the *senpectae,* hungry to learn from their example and grow in recognition of personal limitations.[27] While growing into deepening awareness of who he truly is and is not, the monastic heart is able to admit faults without disparaging self or others.[28] With healthy self-awareness, she loves her prioress and he his abbot—faults and all.

The monastic heart is faithful to the monastic promise professed at the altar and before the praying community, fleshing this out through the daily observance of the monastic way of life.[29] Benedict uses military imagery to paint sober pictures of this reality: daily observance sometimes seems more of a skirmish or all out war than anything simple and peaceful!

We struggle each day to balance work, prayer, rest, play, and the creative.[30] Building a positive community, sustaining and nurturing relationships, building a just and peace-filled world, giving expression to our inner yearnings and insights through creative endeavors, and daily faithfulness to the commitments important to us can at times feel like a draining and futile endeavor. There are many ways we are sustained in our monastic profession. A faith that is grounded in our relationship with God and our faith community reminds us of the purpose of our journey. The stories and memories of the elders in our midst who remind us where we have been helps keep us from discouragement and opens up possibilities for the future. The *senpectae* help us discern where we are in our inner journey and call us into our heritage of hope and joy.

Monastic profession calls the maturing monastic into a nonpossessive relationship with the world: in relationships with others, with material goods, as well as in our emotional life. The monastic receives and uses what is needed for ministry and basic life sustenance but possesses nothing, freely choosing and embracing monastic simplicity.[31] Having freely given self to God in monastic profession, the monastic therefore freely gives up private ownership.[32] The goal is selflessness and joy-filled freedom.[33]

"Living lectio" calls us to reflect on our desires and vision. Do we yearn to make the most of this way of life (rule) that we have chosen as our guide? Is there zeal to learn from our mistakes, and even our successes, in order to be more intentional about our life's goals? Have we recognized the wise persons and mentors available to us? Do we seek connection with these *senpectae*?

Chapter Three

Until It Soaks Into My Bones: Benedict on Prayer

Benedict's Rule is steeped in prayer. It is the fruit of his personal life of an intense practice of prayer. His Rule is designed to lead the beginner into a life of prayer, and in the cultivation of an intense sensitivity of the presence of God, a God Awareness.[1] Benedict allocates times for monastic communal prayer, personal prayer, and lectio. Much of his teaching about other aspects of monastic life assumes a life drenched in prayer. Benedict uses phrases like *every time you begin a good work, you must pray to God most earnestly to bring it to perfection; God is present everywhere; petition . . . with great humility and total devotion; we are heard in purity of heart and tearful compunction . . . prayer should be short and pure, unless perhaps it be prolonged under the inspiration of divine grace.*[2] Benedict exhorts us to approach everything we do with prayer. He encourages us to pray for one another, our leadership, the weak and sick, and the excommunicated. The monastic leader is to pray for the monastics in their charge. Prayer is as necessary and natural as breathing.

Prayer is not simply words we speak to God. Rather it is about standing in the presence of God and listening with a radically open heart. The art or school of prayer is the removal of all— literally all—hindrances within ourselves that keep us from fully entering into God's Presence. God does not withdraw from us; we withdraw from God when we create elaborate walls, detours, and delusions in order to avoid facing God. We fear our emotional and spiritual nakedness, forgetting that we cannot surprise God. We fear the change that is the result of an encounter with God.

Benedictine prayer is basically a *slow-drip method* of transforming into our primordial nakedness before God. Drop by drop, with each momentary experience of God, we slowly let go of the vast distance we have placed between our self and the Holy One. Monastic prayer takes time and persistence and patience. It is a slow immersion into God.

Liturgy of the Hours and lectio divina are the two cornerstones of prayer most closely identified with Benedictine spirituality and the monastic way of life. The Liturgy of the Hours is an ancient form of communal prayer received from the Jewish community. Early Christians, many of whom were Jewish, prayed the psalms and other prayers at set times throughout the day (usually seven different times). These "offices," as they were soon called, marked the rhythm of the day from dawn to deepest night. This was a way of remembering one's utter dependence upon God. The Liturgy of the Hours continues to frame the day so we never drift far from the Source of Life.

Lectio divina, or holy reading, grew out of the desert ascetics' experience of praying the Divine Office. They ruminated on the Word of God in a slow and prayerful way; this led them into quiet and heart-felt prayer. The intent of lectio is a softened, compassionate, and transformed heart that is able to listen intently for the still, small voice of God. Lectio is spiritual formation rather than information gathering. We seek nothing other than the leading of the Holy Spirit in our lives.

In writing his Rule for beginners, Benedict em
basics that must become second nature to us if w
about this way of life and of seeking God. The I
Benedict's thoughtful recommendations for framing
horarium, or daily prayer schedule.

The Liturgy of the Hours

Benedict understood the foundational underpinnings that the Liturgy of the Hours provides for the serious seeker. Opus Dei, or the work of God, was to be the most important part of the day, the focus of our very best attention and energies.[3] His monastics were to exhibit and cultivate eagerness for the Opus Dei.[4] Every other commitment and responsibility was to be quickly set aside when the bells sound for prayer.[5]

Our physical stance during prayer is important. We are embodied creatures; what we do with our body shapes our interior life. Most teachers of lectio, Christian meditation, or centering prayer devote time and energy to how the disciple sits and hold the head. Elements such as posture, rhythm, space, and context ought to be considered and intentionally developed.[6] Monastic liturgists carefully consider how we sit and stand and how we intonate psalms and hymns, constantly stressing the importance of listening to one another.

Attention is given to the creation of sacred space: Changes that reflect particular liturgical seasons, candles, icons, statues and other additions to the praying space, and lighting are each carefully considered.[7] Distractions to the praying community are minimized. Embodied prayer allows us to make connections between all the significant parts of our life and allow these to unfold.

"Living lectio" invites us to explore our God Awareness. In what ways do we stop and notice the movements of the Holy Spirit in our lives? How do we take notice of the radical and unexpected ways that God reveals Sacred Self to us? How do we honor every moment of our lives as a sacred God Moment?

fow are we deepening in mindfulness, that awareness of our presence in the world and of how God is present to us as we are present in the world? How do we notice the difference between self-centeredness and mindfulness? In what ways are we being challenged to deepen our mindfulness? What are our current ascetical practices that support and mature our self-awareness and mindfulness?

How have we created and cultivated sacred space in our lives? This may be a place in our home, places where we walk or jog or bicycle, our favorite fishing spot, or where we go to watch the sun set. Sacred space is where we return repeatedly to be touched by the Divine.

How do we prepare ourselves when we enter our church? How do we internally settle down and bring our best attention to community prayer? Are we aware of how we are in our bodies while at corporate prayer? How might this impact our contemplative interior space?

What balance of private and public prayer have we incorporated into our life? Do we allow for variety in our prayer using meditation, Taizé, biblical prayer, or choosing different translations of the Liturgy of the Hours?

The Psalms

The psalms are ancient prayers of the Israelites. The psalms came out of the lived experience of this praying community, informed by their shared history and communal understanding of the Wholly Other One. They prayed their triumphs and defeats, their courageous acts of compassion and sin, their anger and discouragement, their joy and delight, their transgressions against God and neighbor as well as their moments of reconciliation and atonement. The psalms are real and earthy and ancient.

The psalms are ancient and, for most of us, from a wholly foreign culture and age. We can often find ourselves surprised and offended by what they say. Some of the psalms are meant to jar us and shake us up; some are gifts of comfort. They give voice to hidden parts of us.

In the monastic life, we pray the book of Psalms on a regular and routine basis. The *holy monotony* of praying the psalms each day becomes multifaceted: God speaks to each of us and the full community through particular texts but God also speaks contemplatively at a deeper level that involves no words. Biblical Scholar Irene Nowell reflects:

> What is it that God wants to say to me today through this text? We have a right to expect to hear the voice of God in the psalms—every day. Every day that word will be different—sometimes challenging, sometimes comforting, sometimes the still small sound of silence, sometimes the roar of the devouring fire. Every day, as we listen to the psalms, we listen to the voice of God.[8]

In this stance of receptive expectation, our hearts are ready to engage God in the language God has given us, namely the Psalms.

Biblical scholar Walter Brueggemann points out that the Psalms have the capacity to move the praying community from orientation, through disorientation, and to a new space—a place of reorientation.[9] We experience times of equilibrium; yet when God moves us into a space of dislocation and relocation, the psalms take on a wholly new meaning for us. Words leap out at us; the psalms stir our hearts to be able to hear God speaking to us.

Lament psalms give voice to our raw emotions—in all their chaos, pain, ugliness, and honesty. They teach us to trust God's love for us, and show how we can bring anything, any complaint or event in our life, to One who is able and willing to handle it. Lament psalms also enable us to intercede on behalf of those who find it difficult to continue holding their hands up in prayer and supplication.

Consistent praying of the psalms deepens our self-awareness and moves us toward interior detachment. We can pray, the psalms, bringing our anger and our desire for vengeance, pain, and grief to them. We can trust God to respond in the most loving way.

The psalms invite us to an earthy, real, and embodied experience of prayer. We are challenged to bring before God the full, raw reality of our lives as they really are, not as we think they ought to be.

Contemporary seekers, especially those from the dominant Western Civilization, have difficulty praying some of the psalms.[10] Some monastic communities and other intentionally praying communities have even gone so far as to remove sections of psalms that they find offensive. It is certainly confusing to consider those portions of the psalms that seem violent. How do we contemplatively pray that God *smash the teeth of our enemies*; or *destroy them in your anger, destroy them till they are no more*?[11] It is a jarring experience.

Biblical Scholar Megan McKenna recommends several different ways for us to pray these difficult and unnerving psalms.[12] We can pray these psalms as members of the Body of Christ, sharing in the suffering of those vulnerable to dominant political entities, global mega-corporations, the power-hungry, and the ignorant racists. Unfortunately, the betrayal can run particularly deep when some who call themselves "Christian" are among those inflicting the suffering. We can and ought to pray these psalms together with the suffering, lifting them up before God. Their pain, terror, and horror become ours. In solidarity, we take on the mind and heart of the suffering; the possibility of our own conversion and transformation results.

We pray these psalms in witness and as protest against systemic injustice and greed that inflicts suffering. Members of the dominant culture give voice to those absent (people of color, of non-dominant cultures, the disabled and mentally ill) from our praying assembly and community. The silenced, the ignored, and the oppressed pray these psalms in denunciation of evil, claiming the freedom promised by our Liberating God.

We can pray these hard psalms as *prophetic denunciation* of evil and insensitivity to the plight of the majority of people in this world. This is a prophetic denunciation that hopefully challenges us of the dominant culture to see the injustice that is difficult for us to look at. This is *prophetic memory* for the Church and the world of those who we are called to care for and love in word and action: the crucified and suffering of the earth.

We can enter fully into the emotions expressed in these rough psalms; we can experience the feelings, emotions, and situations as analogous to our own lives. As we pray this way we have the potential to move through pain toward redemption and reconciliation. We risk a heart touched by the suffering of others and we are moved to see the world's reality with new perception.

We can pray these psalms as members of a community and nation examining its conscience. We are invited and challenged to see the ways we have participated in and have been the root cause of this angry, vengeful, mournful, and despairing psalm-prayer; we must take responsibility, do penance, and atone for our collusion with evil. These psalms invite us to mourn for life lost, and for beauty and creation destroyed.

Finally, we can pray these psalms in such a way that our hearts are stretched so that the pain of others becomes our pain as well. Our hearts will be transformed into tender, compassionate, and listening hearts. The horrendous burdens of daily living move us to the core of our being; our life choices begin to change. Our heartfelt response is gratitude and thankfulness for the luxury, richness, and ease of our own lives. We no longer take for granted clean water, abundant food, security, freedom of choice, sleep, healthcare, and freedom from fear of violence. We share out of overwhelming gratitude and abundance.

"Living lectio" invites us to risk facing anger, pain, confusion, and curses through these psalms. We can also write our own psalms of cursing and blessing and yearning. How do we let these psalm texts speak our own stories, unpacking our true feelings and the ways God might be present in the rawness of our lives? How might we risk exploring new images of God based on our honest feelings and God's possible responses to us?

Lectio

The Holy Spirit moves in and through the words of our meditative prayer, providing the living context for wrestling with our own conflicts. Sacred texts are the tools for this interior work. We may be shaken, our self-understanding and self-image challenged and unearthed. Lectio asks of us a listening heart: one that is willing to risk new experiences and possibilities and truth.

Lectio shatters our destructive images of God. Lectio continually reminds us deep in our hearts that our images of God are images; they are not, in themselves, who God is. Lectio undermines our tendencies toward idolatry and makes space for God to reveal the Divine Self to us.

Lectio moves us toward greater intimacy with our truest and most authentic self. As our conflicting attachments are uncovered and healed, interior room is made for a greater awareness of God's presence in our midst. Lectio expands our prayerfulness and consciousness of God.

> The nature of water is soft, that of stone is hard; but if a bottle is hung above the stone, allowing the water to fall drop by drop, it wears away the stone. So it is with the word of God; it is soft and our hearts are hard, but those who hear the word of God often, open their hearts to reverence God (Abba Pimen).

The paradox of lectio is that we can experience it as a waste of time and rewarding at the same time. Most of us do not realize the value of time dedicated to lectio in the immediate present. Rather we become aware of its value indirectly and over time.

The texts we choose for our time of lectio are important because they shape our hearts and minds. Although praying with Sacred Scripture is normative, other texts can be very helpful at different times in our lives: the writings of mystics, the early Church Mothers and Fathers, and contemporary prophets and poets. The Spirit may lead us toward different texts for particular seasons of our life.

Lectio may calm and settle our inner spirit; it may disturb and stir us out of our false contentment. Lectio is the nourishing food of our monastic call to conversion of life. Lectio cultivates in us a reflective stance and presence; we become more sensitive to the movement of the Holy Spirit.

With our commitment to daily lectio, we learn to quietly appreciate that what we give our attention to will soak into our bones.

Whatever we give our attention to touches our heart and consciousness. If we give our time to hours of popular entertainment—
violent and mindless movies, hours of television with its sarcastic
humor and questionable role models, or trashy printed media—
then we can expect our hearts to be cold, hard, and unreflective. If
we feed our mind and soul with poetic and challenging literature,
nourishing movies and television that embrace diversity, staying
engaged with the global news, then we can expect a growing and
compassionate heart. Lectio is active participation in the *divine
dance* allowing the Spirit to lead us. We are invited to listen for the
abundance and gratitude, the oppression, heaviness, and depression around us. We ask: How are we called to respond?

Lectio sharpens our discernment by opening us to the fullness of
life's possibilities, deepening our sensitivity to the leading of the
Holy Spirit, cultivating a heart free to risk, and increasing our
sense of joy. Evelyn Underhill, theologian of mysticism, once said:
*God is not so much interested in nibblers of the possible, rather God is
interested in grabbers of the impossible!* Lectio entices us toward possibilities not previously considered, and empowers us to step out
and risk a dream.

A stance of constant anger or pity or moodiness or despair
moves us away from God; an attitude of openness, gentleness,
flexibility, hope, and peace moves us toward God. This is not to
confuse momentary flashes of anger or sadness with a general disposition toward such attitudes and feelings. We will begin to
notice a transformed inner disposition, an enlivened and genuine
heart, and a resurrection attitude. With lectio, our awareness deepens for those places where we lack the interior freedom necessary
to enter into joy. Ultimately a humble heart is permeable and
receptive to the movements of the Holy Spirit.

Are we paying attention to the texts we are using for our prayer?
Are we meditatively reading sacred scripture, open to the possibility of a transformed heart? Are we distracted with information
and pursuing our curiosity? What effectively helps us move back
from our natural curiosity to formation of heart? Do we discern
our natural curiosity to see if it is inviting us toward new experiences of God? How do we bring our listening hearts to the sacred
texts so that we courageously face the ways we have tamed,

homogenized, and pasteurized sacred texts—taking the sting out of them?

Does our lectio open up new understandings of who God is? Are our metaphors and images of God growing and expanding? Do we bring possibility to our prayer?

Word

Benedict's use of verbs conveys a sense of dynamic movement and urgency, compelling the listener into action. The inner journey was something to be acted upon, not merely contemplated.

Much of our dominant culture is the product of the Enlightenment, which presumes a dualistic, black or white view of the world. This orientation assumes there is one and only one "right" way to approach a situation, solve a problem, or accomplish a task. This approach has been too often applied to the translation and interpretation of sacred texts.[13] This is not the Jewish approach. Jesus, as a devout Jew, suffered under no such limited view. Every text was open to interpretation, and great joy was experienced in openly debating the intent of a word or text.

One of the shortcomings of the rationalist, mechanistic thought habits that arose during the Enlightenment was a distrust of mystery. People sought to explain everything through rationalist thought, or to deny the existence of anything they could not explain. Contemporary American culture has been dominated by this worldview. Basil Cardinal Hume, a Benedictine monastic, wrote that mystery

> lies beyond us, it is too rich for our understanding. It can be entered into, explored, even inhabited; but it can never be exhausted or fathomed. Our age dislikes intensely the idea of mystery, because it directly exposes our limitations. The thought that there could be something, or someone, beyond human comprehension or imagining is, of course, exciting,

but it is also belittling. It puts us in our place and that place is not at the centre.[14]

The monastic way has a tradition around *word* that is different and complimentary to the contemporary parish experience. Our monastic way of life is a lifelong intimate relationship with word. Word for us is not merely what is spoken. Word is like Eucharist: the very living presence of God in our midst. Like Eucharist, word is efficacious and takes on a life of its own. The prophet Isaiah proclaimed of God: *So shall my word be that goes out from my mouth; it shall not return to me empty, but it shall accomplish that which I purpose, and succeed in the thing for which I sent it.*[15] God is present and cannot be contained.

When Moses encountered God in Sinai, he asked God what name he should give the people for God. God was unwilling to be put into a box:

I AM WHO I AM

I WILL BE WHO I WILL BE

I will be gracious to whom I will be gracious.[16]

The monastic heart seeks to avoid these tendencies toward idolatry, of God or of word.

The monastic way is ideally an organic whole. Our lives flow and merge and flow yet again. We do not compartmentalize our lives. We work carefully and meticulously with the proclamation of word. Word is spoken in our lives together and to the world. Word is embraced in our daily practice of lectio where it can seep into hearts, challenging and transforming us.

Word must pierce our hearts, must be ever new, in order to propel and sustain our conversion of life. A word heard repeatedly can lose its edge and cease to speak to us in the same manner. Monastics therefore work very carefully with different translations in order to sustain a fresh and piercing quality. We avoid repetition and redundancies of texts by using many different translations; many monasteries create their own translations.

Benedict tells us:

> Let us open our eyes to the light that comes from
> God, and our ears to the voice from heaven that
> every day calls out this charge: *If you hear God's voice
> today, do not harden your hearts.* And again, *You that
> have ears to hear, listen to what the Spirit says to the
> Churches.* And what does the Spirit say? *Come and
> listen to me and I will teach you the fear of God*
> (Prologue 9–13).

Increasing numbers of seekers are becoming deeply aware of
their hunger and yearning for a regular pattern of prayer in their
lives. They are finding or creating sacred space: a place in their
home, out in the yard, the local park, or a church. Communities are
using one of the Books of Prayer available on the market or creating their own. Many are also connected to a praying community
and even committing themselves as oblates to a religious community. Centering Prayer and Christian Meditation groups support
this call to regular, disciplined prayer when our fast-paced society
tugs and pulls at us.

Is there a goal to monastic prayer? Ultimately, the goal is profound union with God and a world fully reconciled and resurrected. Monastics, lay and vowed, are called to be the crucified Christ
in our world, bearing the burden of suffering and agony until the
fullness of resurrection is realized for all. Our prayer, with the
awareness and transformation that it brings, is the vehicle for
incarnating the crucifixion. There is a prayer that resists the reality of *what is* and envisions a future that God wills for us. Monastic
prayer births forth the possibilities that God desires for us all.

Much happens in a life committed to prayer. Memories, ideas,
and passionate feelings will emerge that may threaten to over-
whelm us. We may grow frightened and confused. We will hit
walls where prayer seems dry and without purpose or meaning.
We may be tempted to give up.

Seekers might explore the ancient Christian tradition of spiritual direction.[17] Spiritual directors are not "experts" with all the
answers to our God-questions. They are fellow students of the

spiritual journey with a gift and call in their lives along with some training. When we journey with a spiritual director, we are choosing to break open together the stuff of our lives in order to discern God's call. Together we can explore frightening emotions, old and painful memories, and all the stumbling blocks in our journey of prayer. We then do not feel so alone or lost or bewildered. Our struggles begin to take on meaning and give form to our path.

Chapter Four

In the Heart of Community: Benedict on Obedience

Obedience is an uncomfortable topic to come to terms with in a postmodern world. Culturally we are in liminal time; we live in a postmodern age that is itself on the threshold of something new.[1] Over the past two hundred years there has been a move from a worldview that placed an omnipotent Creator at the center of the universe (referred to as "premodernity"), to one that placed humanity at the center of the universe ("modernity") and is now fragmented into a loss of any sense of universal meaning ("postmodernity").

The postmodern mind rejects all past frameworks for seeking and defining truth; there is no sense of objective truth that can be sought and understood with any certainty. Now our sense of self is rootless and ungrounded; we feel driven to reinvent ourselves continuously. At the core of our being we feel deeply existentialistic and lost; we feel abandoned in an impersonal cosmos.

The current postmodern worldview perceives life with universal and irresolvable relativism. "Reality" is whatever we decide it should be, and can be redefined anytime that the former definition is inconvenient. There is a lurking sense that neither religion nor the sciences can sufficiently explain a meaningful, unified reality. Theologian Sandra Schneiders, I.H.M., states:

> Reality is just the never-ending, frenetic dance of finite, relative, momentarily connected scraps of existence that are constantly reconfiguring themselves in the cosmic breeze into whatever seems to be or functions as "reality" at the moment. Who is to say that any construction of reality, any set of beliefs or mode of behavior, has universal validity and therefore any claim on me?[2]

We are each free to believe what we want when we want; our beliefs and understandings are our own. However, one's faith with its resulting moral and ethical values and concerns is not welcome in the public realm.[3]

Our postmodern sensibility is deeply aware of a sense of alienation. We are isolated beings cut off from each other. This alienation reflects both an unwillingness and inability to connect with one another in any meaningful and long-term manner. This has led many of us to become apolitical and socially disengaged. We seek to live as distant as possible from the lives and concerns of others, especially of those people who are different. The traditional stories that once served to unite us and explain some elements of our shared life were upended with an awareness of the ways that these stories were limited in who and what was included in the traditioning.

The growing awareness of "otherness" and an increasing awareness of the imperialism that subsumes one culture's story into another has led us to drop these stories completely. Rather than explore these differences, the postmodern, materialistic mind has gone in pursuit of self. If major cultural or sacred stories seemingly contradict one another, then there is no truth or eternal meaning. So "I" becomes the center of my life and a sense of shared reality is lost.

Time, space, and order no longer function as they once did to draw us together and unify us. Due to electricity and the electronic/computer age, we have the ability to choose the time of our day and night. Controlled heat and air-conditioning, advanced technology and communications, and air travel have deeply distorted our former sense of space. We can now be anywhere at any time with any person due to these developments. The corporate world now governs our world. There is now a disorder between our private lives and work; in the meanings of property, community, and commitments; and in what is transitory and what is essential. Anything can be bought, if you have the financial means, at increasingly efficient shopping malls and Internet purchasing sites. We are enslaved to materialism; we are addicted to acquisition. There is never enough.

Scholars and activists have clearly spoken out in profound concern about our destructive self-absorption and materialism. Sexual activity is casual and uncommitted. We are increasingly isolated and vulnerable to destructive addictive tendencies: from exotic new narcotics to mindless sexual activity to a compulsion for the newest and best objects. Our political involvement, when it exists at all, tends to be self-serving rather than stretching, converting, and transforming.

All of us have felt the impact of postmodernity: whether by embracing it to the fullest, energetically trying to reject postmodernism, or struggling to integrate the positive aspects of modernism and postmodernism in some meaningful manner.[4] We must all engage in this cultural shift as "something new yet unknown" emerges.

Without a worldview that supports a sense of human community or eternal truth, we might struggle to understand and relate to the concept of obedience. It would be a grave mistake to throw this concept out. We need to work toward contemporary meaning and significance.

Obedience: Contemporary Concerns

So how do we make meaning out of the concept of obedience? Every generation has its own unique struggles with obedience: ways that we resist and fight it as well as the potential for understanding a spirituality of obedience from a wholly new perspective.

Our postmodern worldview tends to hold "obedience" in disdain. The postmodern mind may have no use for the concept at all; especially a misunderstood concept of obedience. The postmodern mind tends to redefine "obedience" continually and presume this obedience is centered around self; there is little sense of being "bound" by obedience. We would rather think of our obedience as transitory.

Immature obedience can be manipulative, passive-aggressive, complaining, and listless. It is motivated by fear of tyranny or low self-esteem. Obedience grounded in internalized self-hatred drains the family and community of energy and moves the focus away from the heart of the community. This false obedience dwells in a mentality of scarcity rather than the abundance of God.

For those generations that are rugged individualists, there can be a struggle with "no one will tell me what to do" and "only I know what is best for me." For those generations that struggle with trust, obedience would seem impossible. Trust requires a willingness to risk relationship; obedience is always about relationship. There can also be a fear that obedience will crush our creative spirit and limit our unlimited choices.

The early monastic approach to obedience is rich and complex. Obedience was about listening together, discerning the movement of the Holy Spirit in the life of individual seeker and in the community. Obedience was to act upon the word received, committing ourselves to one another and to the communal monastic project.

We normally do not associate obedience with profound freedom or intense joy. For Benedict, obedience is the choice and journey of a mature adult; an obedience that issues forth from our authentic, truest self. Obedience calls forth trust from us that *all shall be well*. Benedict's obedience deepens our self-understanding.

Benedict considered obedience to be grounded in trust and built upon the community listening together *with the ear of their hearts* into discernment. This trust recognizes that the community is able and willing to listen together for God's call and leading, knowing that the Holy Spirit moves within the community. This trustful obedience needs a commitment from each member to intentionally listen within themselves as well as to each other, sharing one's inner journey and sense of God's call.

Mature obedience demands of us a willingness to speak one's truth in trust and then to let go and listen to others. Stepping out in trust to speak our questions, yearnings, and ponderings deepens our self-awareness. Self-awareness is not self-centeredness or selfishness. Self-awareness is a knowledge, understanding, and acceptance of our humanity and of how we are created with gifts and weaknesses and vulnerabilities. A self-centered person lacks honest self-knowledge and other-knowledge. This leads to a disconnect between self and others. There is a post-modern tendency toward creating and sustaining a false public image, putting great energy and resources into sustaining that fantasy.

Obedience, acting on this deep listening from the depths of our heart and from the very core of our being, reveals our attachments: those attitudes, beliefs, and addictions that hold us captive and keep us from freedom. The most difficult attachments to get free from are those that give us some element of joy or security. Faith requires that we let go of these attachments before we discover the intense freedom God desires for us. Obedience guards against self-indulgence and the self-satisfaction that binds us. Deep listening helps us experience interior freedom. We listen to the ways God is calling us—in specific situations and into the future—through one another, our pastor or prioress or abbot, our mentor and wise elder. Deep listening is a kind of living lectio.

Amma Syncletica teaches:

> When we live in community, let us choose obedience over discipline; for the latter teaches arrogance, while the former calls for humility.[5]

The desert ammas experienced the work of listening deeply together and mutual obedience as the place where our interior spiritual journey deepens. Connectedness unmasks the false self and unveils the beauty of our true self. Obedience is about honoring and sustaining mutual connectedness with one another. Mutual obedience does not occur in isolation; but discipline, and especially the practices of "disciplines" such as fasting, could occur in isolation.

What is our history and experience of obedience? What images arise when we hear the word "obedience"? What were some of our positive, life-changing experiences of obedience? Negative experiences? How and what did we learn from these experiences? What helps us grow in trust of our self and others?

Benedict's Rule

Benedict's Rule is permeated with teachings on the monastic tradition around obedience. He begins his Prologue of the Rule with:

> Listen carefully, my child, to my teachings and attend to them with the ear of your heart. Willingly accept the advice of a devoted mentor and put it into action. Thus you will return by the labor of obedience to the Holy One from whom you drifted through inertia and apathy. This message of mine is for you then, if you are ready to renounce self-will, and take up the powerful and shining weapons of obedience to do battle for the Lord Jesus Christ, the true king (Prologue 1–3).

Listen! is the language of Wisdom literature. We are exhorted to listen fully: give complete attention with an open, flexible inner disposition and quick response.[6] *Listening with the ear of our hearts* is listening with the totality of our being: emotions, intuition, intellect, and will. It is the gut-wrenching listening that leads to wisdom and compassion. This compassionate and sensitive listening is the place where we encounter God.[7]

Benedictine scholar Terrence Kardong points out that to listen is the first of four demands for receptivity: listen, attend, accept, and put into action.[8] These commands of response are in the tradition of the desert ascetics who were sought by pilgrims for a word of life: brief, clear, and precise. The word given was savored, considered, and pondered: not easily discarded

To *renounce self-will* may seem undesirable and impossible to us. However this is not a call to deny or suppress our own will.[9] Self-will is the determination to get one's own way, to dominate and control, to live burdened with the belief that one is right (and therefore someone else is wrong). The monastic call to self-awareness deepens our self-knowledge around our will. In this self-awareness we are free to share our knowledge and then let go, trusting the communal process of decision-making.

In the early Christian movement, the phrase *the Lord Jesus Christ, the true King* was a nonviolent statement of resistance to the oppressive political regime. Many died for publicly proclaiming this. This statement meant an individual was rejecting Caesar and choosing Jesus of Nazareth as Lord and King. Treason.

Benedict uses military imagery to color his teaching on obedience. The phrase *fight for*, which can also mean service, is now employed to demonstrate the active nature of obedience as Benedict wanted it exercised by his followers. Obedience is not something to think about and contemplate. Do it! Obey and you will be transformed. Run—the opposite of inertia and apathy—and you will fulfill God's call in your life.

How do we experience listening with the ear of our hearts? What are the warning signals that we have lost touch with this inner place at the center of our being? How do we reflect on and learn from our experiences of deafness? Of not listening? What helps us deepen in awareness of our self-will? In what ways do we listen for what is underneath this self-will that we are trying to protect or hold on to? How do we share this awareness with our wise elders and faith community? Are we nurturing a healthy sense of self? How is listening obedience a way to nurture the self?

✠

> The basic road to progress for the humble person is
> through prompt obedience. This is characteristic of
> those who hold Christ more precious than all else
> (RB 5:1–2).

How seriously do we each take a basic premise of Benedict's: *to hold Christ more precious than all else*? The whole of the monastic journey is about becoming aware of all that keeps us from the most profoundly intimate relationship with the Holy One that is humanly possible. Obedience helps us realize what owns our heart. With this growing self-awareness, we begin to make daily choices according to our deepest values and let our values define and support our choices.

Monastic life is culture shock for all who enter the monastery. New members enter with a life history, which will both support and challenge immersion into the monastic way of life. We come with confidence and a desire for God; but we also bring wounded egos, and a confused and often romantic notion of what the monastic life is all about. Benedict was not interested in rationalization or endless debate. Benedict's Rule requires the beginner to trust the process of immersion and conversion. Do as monastics do and one day you will be a true monastic![10]

Benedict understood that the Christian journey and entrance to a monastery was an excursion into a wholly new culture. One learns to be a monastic by doing monastic things. When we do not understand a practice, a request, or an order from the superior, a mentor or wise elder of the community can be a great help. However, part of learning the monastic way of life is simply to do and then to reflect. Benedict understood this process. Like learning a new sport, a game, or a new language, we must simply try. We can then analyze what went wrong or why something worked correctly, thereby deepening our understanding, but try we must.

Obedience is foundational to the monastic practice. It is the beginning and end of learning the monastic art. *Prompt obedience* reveals the depth of our interior freedom, which moves us toward simplicity rather than unnecessary complexity. This simplicity motivates us to do what we say we will do and be who we say we are; our values are expressed in our actions and choices.

Healthy obedience cultivates an inner and outer responsiveness. In order to be successfully immersed in monastic culture and to learn the monastic way of life, the beginner must be willing to listen and follow instructions. The monastic understanding of obedience is about listening (obedience=listening=act upon listening). Benedict was not interested in perpetuating chronic childhood or chronic dependence or feeding internalized self-hatred. However, he believed that acting upon what has been heard and discerned, whether from God or monastic leader, was intimately connected with spiritual maturity. Benedict understood that a person who walked into the door of the monastery already knowing it all (the *expert*) would fail miserably and cause turmoil within the monastic walls.

In what ways do we hold Christ precious above all else? How are we actively cultivating this passionate love and preference for Christ in our lives?

How do we make choices according to our values and life choices? What do we do when we run into conflicts? How do we exercise prompt obedience without sliding into mindless obedience? How do we actively respond to *a word received*?

✠

On account of the holy service we have professed, as soon as the monastic leader commands something, we waste no time in executing it as if it were divinely commanded.[11] Jesus says of these monastics: *when you heard me, you obeyed me.* Likewise, he says to teachers: *whoever listens to you listens to me.* Such people immediately abandon their own affairs and put aside self-will. We immediately empty our hands, dropping whatever we are doing to carry out with the quick step of obedience the order of the one who commands. It is as if the order was given by the superior and carried out by the disciple at the same instant. Both command and response take place almost simultaneously with an alacrity caused by respect for God. It is love that impels us to progress toward eternal life (RB 5:3–10).

Benedict used the Latin *amor* for love. This is a passionate love—a captured heart—not merely friendly love. This love moves us deeply, changing our very outlook on life and priorities. Benedict was expressing a deep interior motive.

When Benedict speaks of a *love that impels*, several related concepts are at play here. There are two possible translations: one more literal than the other.[12] To impel is a rapid forward movement: therefore, to listen is to respond. Love is the propulsion, the energy force, or the motivation to stay with the inner journey no matter how difficult or painful this interior work may become.

There is value in the literal translation of the phrase *love of progressing*. When we passionately desire something, we find creative ways to make it happen and we are thrilled as we draw closer and closer to our goal. While love may be a part of our motivation for the hard work of growth, awareness that we actually are growing and becoming more free gives us the vision and hope to keep on going. Our goal is joy and intense freedom.

Self-will is a form of stubborn willfulness. This is different from one's own personal will, preferences, wishes, or desires. Our personal will is grounded in who God created us to be: our true self. Our personal will is deeply connected to our conscience. We cannot set aside our personal will as this would mean denying our individual existence. The monastic call is toward self-awareness through which our personal will would become increasingly familiar to us.

Self-will is attached to personal preferences and demands. When we act out of self-will, we can be manipulative, deceptive, and controlling. Self-will is closed to life, to others, to community and family. It undermines the fabric of family and community life.

Benedict teaches that authentic obedience softens our strong self-will. The Rule calls us to self-awareness, to continually form our consciences and to know our personal desires. In mature obedience, we are free and self-confident enough to let go of our personal preferences toward the heart of the monastic community. We are literally cultivating the practice of putting on the Mind of Christ.

Benedict contrasts prompt obedience to sloth and mindlessness.[13] Mindlessness comes from a reluctance to assume responsibility for one's own life or from fear or other psychological impairments. Sloth is laziness and a lack of engagement with life. Both are enemies of the interior journey and monastic way of life.

Eager response reveals that our hearts are rooted in community. Benedict's phrases *dropping whatever we are doing* and *the order was given and carried out in the same instance* disclose a deeply listening heart that understands the needs and priorities and goals of the community; therefore response can be quick and simple. It indicates a listening and obedient disposition that is able to respond quickly.

Benedict was seeking an obedience that has been interiorized and not mere external conformity. This is thinking, intelligent obedience. Mature obedience is internal as well as external. While we begin to learn the monastic way through imitation, our inner journey deepens and we grow in wisdom when we have internalized obedience. We are listening and prayerfully reflecting upon all that life is teaching us.

Internalized obedience implies a healthy sense of self and also supports our growth into a healthier sense of self. We are secure enough to share our wisdom and insights and to then let go and trust the outcome. This is a self that is strong enough to trust the heart of community to make the best decisions humanly possible. This is a self that knows the Holy Spirit has not abandoned us.

As we internalize obedience our heart is shaped into the heart of community, trusting that our heart is becoming the heart of Christ. We serve one another as colleagues, equals, and partners, not out of fear, a need to control others and events, or a sense of worthlessness. Benedict is interested in attitude, not just efficiency. Sometimes the "quick response" of obedience takes the form of prayerful discernment and holy conversation with the monastic leader.

What helps us become aware of our own experiences of self-will and stubbornness? What enables us to become aware of and acknowledge our personal will and desire? Are we bringing these to our spiritual director or mentor? In what ways are we cultivating an intense love for God?

✠

> Therefore we seize on the narrow way, of which Jesus says: *the route that leads to life is narrow*. That is why we do not wish to live by our own lights, obeying our own desire and wants. Rather, we prefer to walk according to the judgment and command of another, living in cenobitic community with a superior over us. People such as these imitate Jesus, who said: *I did not come to do my own will, but the will of the One who sent me* (RB 5:11–13).

The *narrow way* for Benedict is monastic obedience. It is the intense listening that deepens our awareness of the movement of the Holy Spirit in our lives and in the life of our community. When we seize on the narrow way, we have taken ownership for the monastic way of obedience to the point of anticipating needs and direction with zeal. This is NOT unhealthy co-dependence where we might be seduced into taking care of others, or inflicting unwanted assistance upon them. Rather, this is healthy team playing, in the way professional athletes so know and understand each other that they can effectively anticipate moves and strategies. This is the self-motivated person who conscientiously hustles to see a project to a quick and effective completion. This is the person who goes the extra mile without being asked and is motivated by the joy and satisfaction of what she is doing.

The narrow way is unique to each of us. Jesus and the Holy Spirit call, we respond. Yet within that salvific call is an invitation that is uniquely personal. The narrow way must be discerned with mentors and those with whom we have a commitment. Matthew 11:30 tells us that *our yoke is easy and our burden light*. Those who work with animals would tell us that each ox has its own yoke and that yoke is never switched. The leather is worked to fit to each particular animal—a custom fit. This way the ox is not harmed in the process of hard labor.

With our baptism, we begin to make choices that define our narrow way. Hopefully we discern major life decisions with the help of wise family members and friends, as well as our spiritual mentor. As we faithfully follow the lead of the Spirit, our yoke becomes custom fit for us; it is uniquely ours. Marriage, family, ministry, faith community, or the call to religious life clearly brings distinction to our narrow way. Our call then is to be faithful to this narrow way and allow it to become our teacher and our asceticism.

For monastics, the narrow way includes the monastic promise and its demands on our daily choices, the particular monastery where we have laid our written promise, and the monastic leader. On this path even the crazy things that happen in daily life become our way of salvation. For married people, the narrow way is shaped by devotion to a spouse, commitment to children, and involvement with the faith community.

Kardong sees the phrase, *prefer walking according to the judgment and commands of another,* as the structural core of Benedict's views on obedience.[14] The narrow way of Christ and the Cross is to live under obedience, which is the movement toward resurrection. Obedience is a response to our spiritual leader (prioress, abbot, pastor, mentor) and to our community of commitment (the monastery for the monastic and oblate). Be discerning and prudent in choosing your mentors, who must be wise and compassionate. Once we know and trust our leader and community, we incarnate our commitments through mutual obedience. Benedict is addressing the *lone rangers*, the "experts" who have all the answers. He wants to move us from the tyranny of extreme individualism.

Cenobitic obedience is always understood within the context of community. The context of community serves to dismantle any emerging tyranny from the leader, an individual member, or a group within the community. It is a heart so grounded in the heart of community that *doing my own thing* seems repugnant.

Wise monastics value effective mentoring relationships; learning by doing and then sharing about the experience with a mentor to learn how to improve our performance and reach our goals. A wise mentor or elder can help us unpack experiences to discover the hidden and unconscious drives that separate us from our true self. Benedict is again addressing the strength and gift of working as a team: A valuable team player can really hear the other members of the team.

The community, be it family, committed faith community, or monastery, must discern together how God is calling. We must set our hearts within the very heart of the community, a heart-to-heart connection. We seek a heart so grounded in the heart of community that *doing my own thing* seems distasteful. Cenobitic obedience is always understood within the context of community. This guards against tyranny of the prioress, a spouse or child, or any individual or small group within the community.

Do we know our own *narrow way*? Is this path becoming familiar and comfortable? Why is there resistance? What do our fears and anxieties tell us? Are we committed? Do we trust the process? The journey? What supports our journey away from extreme individualism toward interconnectedness and commitment? How are we listening for the life-giving aspects of our yoke and how it impels us toward love? How are we digging for the wisdom to be unearthed?

✠

> But this same obedience will only be acceptable to God and humanly attractive if the command is not executed fearfully, slowly, or listlessly, nor with murmuring or refusal. For obedience given to monastic leaders is given to God, who said: *Whoever listens to you, listens to me*. And it should be given gladly by disciples, for God loves a cheerful giver. If a disciple obeys grudgingly and murmurs not only out loud but also internally, even if the order is carried out, it will not be acceptable to God. For God sees the heart of the murmurer, who will receive no thanks for such a deed. On the contrary if the monastic does not make satisfaction, the penalty of murmurers will be received (RB 5:14–19).

Power issues were alive and thriving in Benedict's day just as they are in ours. Mumbling, dragging our feet, and uncaring or frightened responses are a misuse of our God-given power. Mumbling, grumbling, and murmuring are power plays: we may technically do what we are asked but we will be certain that everyone around us suffers for it.

Mumbling is an elusive evil that subverts communication and the community discernment process; it's a creeping discontent. Mumblers are seeking domination and control, tending to believe that they know it all and certainly know what is best for the family or community. Mumbling undermines the woven fabric of community and family. Murmuring is an act of denial of our God-given narrow way and, for monastics, of the monastic promise made before the community. It betrays an ungrateful heart, presuming we deserve better. It denies God's gift of freedom.

Healthy obedience does not diminish self or others. Rather, it calls forth life, supporting and enlivening the heart of community. Benedict's obedience teaches our modern sensibility the gift of trust. Working through difficulties and challenges with one another, even the person we tend to consistently disagree with, teaches a heart-centered trust.

Obedience honors and supports one's personhood, while also challenging each monastic to form their individual consciences. It does not diminish the individual or violate a person's conscience. Our self-will, stubbornness, mumbling, misuse of power, rebellion—all that disrupts the monastic observance—are confronted through a healthy and proper understanding of obedience.

Authentic discernment happens within a committed community and by individuals with informed consciences. The paradox is that obedience builds the authentic strength of the person: Trust and discernment turn power, as our modern culture popularly understands power, on its ear. Our struggle is to be grounded in the knowledge of personal will and God's Will. We must know our own will and conscience in a particular matter in order to appropriately respond in quick obedience. Benedict's obedience is about the quality of our responsiveness.

Our motive for obedience is awe and respect and reverence for God, loyalty to Christ, and respect for each other. Obedience is the path of returning to God. We obey Christ and we obey like Christ: We are seeking to be Christ to the world.[15] We are letting our hearts be shaped into the heart of God. The hard and honest work of obedience leads to a compassionate heart.

The Benedictine call is to mutual obedience: within community, family, parish faith community, and the mentors and wise elders God has placed in our life. Obedience teaches us to trust the process of growth that the Holy Spirit has invited us in engage in. When we practice obedience and work to cultivate a listening compassionate heart, we begin to identify our true friends. Obedience is grounded in relationship and further builds relationship; mutual obedience means *I care.*

How are we cultivating a healthy relationship with our personal power? Do we listen to our mumbling, grumbling, and complaining to see what is pushing to be unearthed? In what ways do we speak truth to our power? To our denial of personal power?

✠

> When someone newly comes to the monastic life, easy entrance should not be granted.
>
> We must note whether the newcomer really seeks God, shows eagerness for the Work of God, obedience, and hardships.
>
> The one to be received into the community must promise stability, fidelity to the monastic way of life, and obedience before all in the oratory (RB 58:1, 7, 17).

These verses are from Benedict's chapter on the procedures for accepting new members. The process for discerning, testing, and accepting potential new monastics was already well established by Benedict's time. He added a few innovations but remained firm in the monastic tradition. The presumption is that anyone who comes knocking on the monastery door, hears the reading of Benedict's *Rule,* and requests admission is aware that obedience to the monastic way of life is the heart of the monastic promise.

Mutual obedience is needed for effective discernment. Discernment is accomplished through the wisdom of committed community. The seekers' community of discernment may include a spiritual director, a mentor, a spouse, family, and close friends. The process of discernment involves the seeker and wise elders responsible for formation. The monastic tradition recognizes the inevitable challenges to the spiritual journey. An intentional seeker who wants to focus on the interior journey must have sufficient interior strength for monastic life. Wise elders discern with the seeker to ascertain whether basic skills are present to live the monastic life, to face interior and exterior challenges in a healthy manner, and to thrive with joy.

Learning a new way of life is not easy. Nor is learning who we really are. Healthy obedience keeps us to the task of learning our *narrow way* and not trying to slip our personalized yoke off. Like the sacrament of Matrimony, the monastic promise moves this journey away from one's self out into the community. This is our journey *together,* not merely one's own.

How do we listen to the internal resistances to life? How are we unpacking the wisdom behind interior resistance? In what ways are we discerning whether resistance is a call to change or a sign of our attachments and self-will? How are we seeking God? Is joy present?

✠

> If it should happen that some heavy or impossible tasks are given to us, we should accept the order with all gentleness and obedience. If we see that the weight of the task altogether exceeds our strength, we should patiently point out to our superior why we cannot do it. We should do so at the proper time, and without pride, obstinacy, or refusal. If our monastic leader's mind remains unchanged, we should realize it is in our best interest. Then, confident in the help of God, we must lovingly obey (RB 68).

The root word in Latin for *accept* is the same as the one used in RB 58, the *suscipe* of monastic profession or oblation. As we in faith seek God's acceptance of our monastic profession, so we accept our superior's requests in faith. This is not a mindless acceptance, but rather an intelligent and dynamic acceptance that things will work out. We may need to seek clarification of a request made to us. This needs to be done from a place of humility that knows our strengths and weaknesses while acknowledging that we have untapped abilities.

Benedictine scholar Aquinata Böckmann points out that Benedict begins this chapter with a call to prompt obedience and concludes with an informed response of obedience.[16] This happens as a result of our struggle to know God's Will for us. In following the progression of adverbs used, we see Benedict's requirement of increasing maturity until love is reached.

There are times when we may be asked to do something that seems impossible. Our monastic leader may have forgotten or never known our lack of talent or training in some area. It would be a kindness for us to remind leadership of this. However, our monastic leader may be aware of some innate and untapped talent we possess and decide to call this untested talent forth. The limitations of small communities sometimes necessitate unusual requests. Benedict allows for conversation: open, nonbelligerent, and gracious. In the end, our monastic heart in loving obedience calls us to do as we are asked, trusting the outcome.

Often life hands us impossible situations and impossible tasks. How do we respond when faced with these? In what ways do we incorporate our mentor or discerning community into the process of facing these daunting situations?

✠

The blessing of obedience is not only something that everyone ought to show the monastic leader, but we should also obey one another. We know that we will go to God by this path of obedience. Therefore, except for an order of the monastic leader, which we permit no private command to override, all juniors must obey their seniors with every mark of loving attention. But if any of us is found resistant in this matter, we should be rebuked. If, however, any of us is rebuked for the slightest reason by the monastic leader or any senior in any way whatsoever, and if we see that any senior at all is even faintly perturbed at us or disturbed in any way, we should instantly prostrate on the floor at their feet to make satisfaction and remain there until the disturbance has been healed by a blessing (RB 71:1–8).

Benedict began with an admonition that monastics practice mutual obedience. He further explored mutual obedience in the following chapter. The Prologue to the Rule began with an admonition to the labor of obedience. Benedict then concluded with the blessings of obedience. As cenobitic obedience is internalized, it becomes a blessing in myriad ways.[17]

Benedict's mutual obedience is closely linked to today's language around having a self-in-relation. Scholars and educators have recognized that women thrive in relationships, whether personal or professional, that are based on interdependence and relationality. Mutual obedience is a commitment to connectedness and relationship. This is never meant to diminish or eliminate a healthy sense of self. Self-in-relation is affirmed and strengthened by mutual obedience. Benedict's *path of obedience* refers to the monastic way and its tradition of seeking God. It is a dynamic journey that recognizes the mutually supportive interplay between obedience and spiritual maturity.

When Benedict speaks of mutual obedience with *every mark of loving attention*, he reminds us of the quality of relationship between mentor and seeker. Much like his admonition to *listen with the ear of our hearts*, we bring an open and receptive heart to mutual obedience. Every encounter has the potential for learning. This is the ideal stance when we enter into a spiritual direction relationship. It would be counterproductive for us to seek out a spiritual director and then immediately begin to argue with every word given and every question asked!

Mutual obedience as a spiritual discipline leads us to seek reconciliation and resolution in difficult situations. We are to *make satisfaction*, that is, to persist until the conflict has been cleared up. It implies that we are open to being wrong. Others who are wounded or sinful may not be able to accept resolution. It would not be healthy to presume that those of us lower in rank are responsible for all rifts in relationships; regardless of blame, we must quickly extend respect to the other.

How do we understand mutual obedience? How do we seek to improve communication? Fight fairly? Seek resolution? Do we courageously speak what is on our hearts without using our words as "weapons of war"?

✠

Just as there is an evil and bitter zeal that separates us from God and leads to hell, so too there is a good zeal that separates us from evil and leads to God and eternal life. Thus we should practice this zeal with the warmest love: *let us all strive to be the first to honor one another.* We should bear each other's weaknesses of both body and character with the utmost patience. We must compete with one another in obedience. We should not pursue what we judge advantageous to ourselves, but rather what benefits others. We must show selfless love to one another. Let us fear God out of love. We should love our monastic leader with sincere and humble charity. Let us prefer absolutely nothing to Christ, and may he lead us all together to everlasting life (RB 72).

Zeal is an exceptional fervor and enthusiasm that motivates us through the difficult times of the spiritual journey that are inevitable. Living in community and giving our heart, mind, and focus to that community is challenging. Foibles, imperfections, and simple human clumsiness can disrupt our best efforts and intentions. Zeal and *fervent love* for God and the monastic way keeps us steadily on course.

While the first obedience in the monastic way is to our superior, mature obedience is grounded in passionate respect for all. Mutual obedience is expressed in *warmest love, bearing each other's* weaknesses, *utmost patience, tolerance, honor, deference,* and *sincerity.*

Are we still excited about the spiritual journey? How do we savor and preserve our vision and goal? In what ways do we deepen our love and tenderness for those to whom we are committed? How do we protect and nurture our monastic hearts?

Chapter Five

Humility:
Contemporary Considerations

Benedict's Rule contains a famous chapter on humility that has formed the basis for both traditional theology and mystical theology. Historically, Benedict's teachings have, at times, been grossly misunderstood and misused to justify a rather negative view of humanity. His teachings on humility have also been foundational to understanding the interior and mystical journey. Contemporary spirituality is rediscovering the gems to be found in Benedict's words, while recognizing that there are problematic sections.

Monastics traditionally understood humility to be deeply valuable to the spiritual journey. Wise elders of the desert and monastic traditions tried to instill in their followers a healthy appreciation for this virtue. Humility was experienced as the vehicle for experiencing God's love and joy.

✠

> Holy Scripture cries out to us, saying: *Whoever is self-promoting will be humbled, and whoever is humble will be promoted*. When the heart is humble, the Holy One raises it up to heaven (RB 7:1, 8b).

Humility is not an especially popular word today, nor is it well understood. At the mere mention of the word, we may encounter responses of repugnancy, dismay, or even surprise that some consider this a contemporary concern. We may hear pious platitudes about the importance of humility, and then get the uneasy sense that this devout person has never really wrestled with the concept.

Humility is about being really real, and thus deeply aware of the Wholly Otherness of God. It is a journey from that public persona we have built up in our early adult years toward that true *self* made in the image and likeness of Christ. Humility is the fruit of letting go of all the interior stuff that weighs us down, distracts us from our life's passions and goals, and keeps us from a simple and empowering relationship with God. Humility is a grace and gift freely given to us by God.

Jesus personified a healthy humility. He showed by living example, as well as through his teaching and preaching of the Kingdom of God, the life-giving power of humility. Jesus was able to embody authentic humility that affirmed the dignity of the human person in the eyes of God and defied the cultural norms of his day.

Early Christian writers, such as Amma Syncletica, Evagrius Pisone, Ponticus, and Cassian taught about cultivating the virtue of humility with the pitfalls to be encountered when maturing in humility.[1] Later, the Master and Saint Benedict based their teachings on humility on these earlier traditions.[2]

Benedict's chapter on humility uses language and imagery that, when misunderstood, can be truly harmful to our interior journey. Some troublesome phrases include *fear of God; obedient to the point of death; when obedience involves harsh, hostile things . . . one embraces them patiently; content with low and dishonorable treatment; I am a worm, not human; it is good for me that you humiliate me;* and *constantly aware of guilt for sins*. These ideas run contrary to our cultural understanding of human worth. Many people grow concerned and even get angry when encountering these images, which tend to perpetuate shame, guilt, and unhealthy images of God.

Benedict's Ladder of Humility

Both the Master and Benedict use the image of a ladder with angels ascending and descending to denote the early monastic understanding of growth in virtue.[3] The ladder is very linear and hierarchical; the image is very limiting. I find the image of a helix to be more helpful in understanding the inner dynamic of interior growth.[4] The spiritual journey is not linear; we revisit our fragility, vulnerability, sin, strengths, and God's call in our life repeatedly. The helix twists and turns and dances, reminding us that as we deepen in interior freedom and humility, we are still beginning anew.

Despite all our individual and corporate attempts at self-sabotage, conscious or unconscious, a basic inner yearning and drive toward our most whole self and union with the Divine remains. We yearn to come home to ourselves and to God. The Spirit within constantly entices us further in the journey toward humility. In applying "the new science" to the world of business, Margaret Wheatley reminds us that

> Everything is in a constant process of discovery and creating. Everything is changing all the time: individuals, systems, environments, the rules, and the processes of evolution. Even change changes. Every organism reinterprets the rules, creates exceptions for itself, and creates new rules. Life uses messes to get to well-ordered solutions. Life doesn't seem to share our desires for efficiency or neatness. It uses redundancy, fuzziness, dense webs of relationships, and unending trials and errors to find what works.[5]

This new science teaches us that life makes sense and continually seeks meaning.

> Life is in motion, "becoming becoming." The motions of life swirl inward to the creating of self and outward to the creating of the world. We turn inward to bring forth a self. . . . Life takes form from such ceaseless motions. But the motions of life have direction. Life moves toward life. We seek for connection and restore the world to wholeness.[6]

We yearn for a deeper and more profound experience of life. This yearning propels us in the search.

We resist imposed processes that have been generated in another time or context. This resistance is an instinctive honoring of the inner creativity God has gifted us with. We do not so much resist change as we resist an imposition of change from outside our inner processes. Wheatley speaks of this as a resistance of a living system to being treated as a nonliving thing. We assert our inherent tendency to seek our truest self.

Women and Humility

Traditional teachings on the virtue of humility arose out of the experiences of men. While several early *ammas* and monastic women had their own teachings on humility, they were, like their male counterparts, still heavily influenced by the Greek suspicion of the human body that had its roots in a dualistic and patriarchal worldview.[7] Today we are able to benefit from the research and wisdom of recent decades on the unique needs and gifts that women bring to their monastic journey. A woman's journey into humility has different nuances. There are two specific issues that need to be addressed in a woman's journey toward humility: a woman's sense of self and her relationship to power.

Women cannot give up a self they do not possess. A woman's journey into humility begins by discovering that she has a self and who this self is. Then she must struggle to live from this self. As natural connectors and builders of community, women make this journey as a *self-in-relation*. Personality development theorists speak of the process of our maturing being one of dependence to independence to interdependence. This self-in-relation recognizes the importance of human community for our survival, as well as our happiness. Self-in-relation requires that we have a self to bring to community, and it acknowledges that we know ourselves because of our relationships with others.

Patriarchal cultures tend to undermine any person's sense of self, as the perpetuation of patriarchy requires a false public self. Any person growing in their authentic, true self is a threat to patriarchal systems. Due to the effects of patriarchy, a woman's journey into humility requires that she first discover who she is as distinct from the person patriarchy told her that she is.[8] For many women, this is a painful and lifelong struggle.

Theologian Carol Ochs speaks of the traditional language of "dying to the self" as "de-centering the self," meaning focusing away from "the narcissistic, individualistic egocentric self that cares for others out of its own need."[9] A woman's journey toward humility is about discovering and accepting the person created in the Divine image, therefore embracing her value and importance before God.

Jesus lived the right use of power. Repeatedly he tried to show, through story and by personal example, how to use one's empowering use of God-bestowed power. For example, we read in Luke's gospel: *If anyone strikes you on the cheek, offer the other also; and from anyone who takes away your coat do not withhold even your shirt.*[10] The Roman era had clearly defined and enforced class distinctions: who could interact with whom and how one was expected to behave. When a person from a higher class struck someone from a lower class, the appropriate response was to hang one's head. When an equal struck an equal, the appropriate response was to turn the other cheek, signifying equality of class. Jesus was challenging his followers to claim their dignity. This is a mutually respectful response, not retaliative or vindictive. One does not strike back at the enemy or cooperate with any diminishment. Our response comes from a place of dignity and inner freedom.

Benedict learned from hard experiences with difficult community members. He was aware of power dynamics and how these could build or destroy the monastic community. In writing his *simple rule for beginners*, Benedict was attempting to shift power relations by addressing root causes of power distortion and framing a communal way of life that brings correctives to the behavior of "little tyrants."

The complexity of power issues is becoming increasingly clear. Pastors, attorneys, educators, medical professionals, clergy, and mental healthcare professionals are all very powerful people over the lives of those entrusted to them. Families can have one or more members who wield power over the rest of the family and be unaware of it.

In exploring a woman's struggles with a healthy sense of self and power, I hope to unpack these hard teachings in Benedict's writings on humility in light of the best of contemporary social sciences.

In Search of a SELF

Women have traditionally struggled to develop a sense of self and to embrace that self as genuinely worthy. Pastoral Theologian Carroll Saussy defines the self as

> body, mind, and spirit; abilities and limitations; and repressed and remembered experiences both positive and negative; bodily experience, relational experience, cultural experience, religious experience. People are themselves, some combination of true self—that is, the unique aliveness experienced at the deepest level of the human psyche, hinting at the realistic possibilities of who they might become—and false self, either an idealized image

others have held up to them as to who they ought to be or a negative image of the failure others have predicted they will become.[11]

For some women, it is a greater challenge to embrace their truest self; it is far easier to deny self.

Educational Psychologist Robert Kegan has challenged the more traditional and male-based theories of personality development. He broadened these approaches by incorporating aspects of human development traditionally ignored—affective, cognitive, meaning-making, and social development—into his theory. He created an active and evolving model that he calls the "helix of evolutionary truces." Kegan states that there are "periods in our life when the terms of our evolutionary truce must be renegotiated. These terms are the self. Their renegotiation is a natural emergency."[12] We live with a tension between yearning for independence or autonomy and yearning for inclusion. These yearnings seem to be in conflict; there is a tension in their relation with one another. Kegan suggests that this lifelong tension—always slightly unbalanced in favor of one yearning over the other and yet moving back and forth—results in an experience of this fundamental ambivalence that makes up the unitary, restless, creative motion of life itself.

Classical developmental frameworks have univocally defined growth in terms of the traditionally male attributes of differentiation, separation, and increasing autonomy. They tended to ignore traditionally feminine attributes of integration, attachment, and inclusion. Educational Psychologist Carol Gilligan has pointed out that integration was often spoken of in terms of dependency and immaturity.[13]

The importance of Kegan's work for women's growth into humility is that his work values interdependent relationship, community, and interior detachment, which are all monastic values. We humans are not linear beings. Our growth will involve "revisiting" past issues at new and deeper levels, and also journeying forth into new territory. The self naturally seeks out and listens to information that might cause it to alter behavior. An interior freedom grows and develops as one detaches from objects, institutions, and relationships even while being in the midst of them. Interior freedom is a mediating relationship—a dynamism, flow, or play—that results from the capacity of the newly emerging self to move back and forth between psychic systems within the self.

Kegan developed a helix model for his stages of personality development.[14] These stages, called evolutionary truces, are "incorporative," "impulsive," "imperial," "interpersonal," "institutional," and "interindividual."[15] Kegan's interindividual self is the stage where we can share with others without losing our self. The capacity for intimacy with others springs from our capacity to be intimate with our self. We are *beings-in-relation* rather than "having" relationships; we do not possess others, nor are we possessed by others. The other extreme of isolation does not occur either.

Shame, a common human experience, thwarts healthy discovery of self. Writer Elizabeth Horst speaks of shame as "a feeling that interrupts other, positive feelings, and in doing so it produces a global, negative evaluation of the self. Shame is the internal voice that hisses, 'Stop that! You're bad!' In subjective experience shame is the sure and certain knowledge that you are completely flawed, defective to the core, deserving of nothing except to disappear."[16] Shame is an inner feeling of diminishment and insufficiency. It is insidious and elusive in its power to bind and oppress us. Horst writes:

> The power of shame to undermine the victim's sense of self, her capacity to love and accept herself, and her capacity for genuinely giving and receiving love seriously erodes her capacity for religious belief and a healthy spirituality. Shame engenders deep estrangement within the self and between the self and others—and sometimes between the victim and God.

Later, Horst reminds us that

> sexual abuse is particularly destructive for spirituality because the locus of violation and shame is the

body itself. Alienation from one's bodied self is crip-
pling for any experience of spirituality because spirituality is rooted in a sense of connectedness with
those forces that give and sustain life. It involves a
sense of meaning and the possibility for life that is
larger than one's own efforts.[17]

The artificial de-humanizes and de-natures us by making us
appear what we are not, keeping us from our center, Christ. In the
monastic tradition, we seek the authentic and embrace our vulnerability. We speak of discovering and uncovering a true self and
shedding a false self. Pastoral Theologian Carroll Saussy refers to
the false self as the

> adapted self who lives according to other people's
> expectations. The false self accommodates to
> parental needs, losing touch with authentic wants
> and needs, and is rewarded for making the adapta-
> tion. [Psychotherapist Alice] Miller calls the false
> self an "as-if personality" that keeps the true self in
> a state of noncommunication. The true self, elusive
> because it is always in the process of becoming,
> begins to emerge with the authentic expression of
> feelings, sensations, and needs, which later become
> the authentic expression of ideas and emotions. The
> primitive capacity to feel one's needs and communi-
> cate them is the earliest sense of self, one's "experi-
> ence of aliveness."[18]

Margaret Wheatley's work with the new science can be helpful
in our understanding of women's growth. It acknowledges and
affirms the messiness of life, growth, and relationships, reminding
us that chaos has order in it. In her book, *A Simpler Way*, Wheatley
says,

> People are intelligent, creative, adaptive, self-organ-
> izing, and meaning-making. Life self-organizes. Life
> organizes around a self. Organizing is always an act

of creating an identity. The universe is a living, creative, experimenting experience of discovering
what's possible at all levels.[19]

We naturally yearn for growth. Communities and families provide
the context, fodder, and fertilizer for this growth.

Wheatley tells us that the self changes when it expands its consciousness about itself. As the self develops a different awareness,
this changed awareness will materialize as new responses. Change
and growth are the result of increased self-awareness. Self-
reflection is the fertile ground for change.

Our emerging sense of self may be brought to "living lectio."
Here we can face the destructive messages and images inflicted
upon us. We can challenge the lies we may have lived out. Here,
too, we can hear God speak the truth about our inherent value. We
can discover the positive messages about our self that gave us
courage to risk the challenges of life.

What kinds of internal names do we give ourselves? How
would we honestly describe who we are? In what ways are we
being called to focus and grow in our sense of self? What blocks
are we currently aware of that hinder a healthy sense of self? What
positive and negative messages have we internalized about who
we are or who we are *supposed* to be? What effectively helps us
continue to assess and work with maturing in our sense of self?
How do we express, or fail to express, our *being-in-relation*? Are we
isolated or deeply connected?

Power Issues

Every human is powerful, pulsating with life force. From the time
of conception, when we announced our immanent arrival with a
cry, to the season late in life when we assert ourselves with family
or the nursing home staff, we have used our personal and public
power. Power is essential to who we are as humans. Even beyond
the grave we continue to exert our power!

Women have tended toward an ambivalent relationship with power. Power is often seen as a negative and destructive force in relationships. Oftentimes we have experienced misuse of power through oppressive control or inappropriate expressions of anger. Our culture tends to respond to anger with feelings of dread and denial. Anger, which Carroll Saussy defines as a response to the experience of being ignored, injured, trivialized, or rejected, is an expression of power; this experience of anger exposes our innate sense of diminished worth and our life force (power).[20] Suppression of anger leads to depression and women tend toward a higher rate of depression than men do.

Jean Baker Miller, M.D. defines power as the capacity to produce a change. This can include thoughts, emotions as well as the interpersonal fields of politics, economics or the social realm. Women tend to be more comfortable empowering others but not exercising power ourselves.[21] We fear that to exercise power is selfish and destructive; we fear that if we use our power with efficacy, freedom, and joy, others might abandon us.

I believe the real fear for many women is that the power that harmed us may be the full and exclusive definition of power. We have been silenced, diminished, or manipulated by power. Too many women, as children and as adults, have been sexually violated. By the first grade, little girls know that "the world" is unsafe and they need to be aware. Unfortunately, when an assault does occur, this child presumes it is her fault and she grows up with guilt and shame. Women have historically been forced to accept sexual harassment at work and in the Church, knowing full well who holds the power over her job, her access to the sacraments, and her world.

We are increasingly aware of the scandal of sexual misconduct by presidents, pastors, teachers, lawyers, and doctors. Those who hold places of authority in society have violated the trust of those they serve through significant boundary violations.

> Power dynamics, where there is an investment in personal ascendancy or dominance of one person over another, clearly interfere with mutuality . . . if one is primarily concerned with the establishment

of a position of dominance vis-à-vis another, that motive eliminates the possibility of a real interest in the subjective experience of the other. Rather, one's own interests are felt as uppermost.[22]

As women who value connection, community, and mutuality, we do not want to exercise destructive power so we are inclined to deny that we have any power at all.

We may have heard numerous times and in a variety if situations, "I am not powerful. I am helpless," and known deep within ourselves how wrong that claim was. Some of the most powerful people we may encounter—not necessarily empowering, just powerful—will staunchly deny their power. Since each of us is powerful, the only question is our self-awareness of where our power is and how we are using it. When we claim "I have no power" we are abdicating responsibility for our choices and actions. When we are not open and free with our personal power we act out in other ways. Then "powerlessness" expresses itself in passive-aggressive behavior, depression, rage, and attempts at earning pity from others for our alleged helplessness.

Healthy power is connected to our sexuality and generativeness. It is an integral force that allows us to connect with others intimately in intimacy, friendship and mutuality. It includes our ability to attract others into our life: parents, teachers, friends, and significant others. Power enables us to give life, to gift the world with our creativity, insights, and contributions. Theologian Rita Nakashima Brock refers to this as erotic power "grounded in the relational lives of women and in a critical, self-aware consciousness."[23] Erotic power builds "relationships of self-awareness, vulnerability, openness, and caring. Eros is not about control; it is about connection with our whole selves and the selves of others."[24] Erotic power "dissolves the alienation which has overly compartmentalized our lives and it emerges as a sensuous, transformative whole-making wisdom that engages our whole heart in relational contexts."[25] Eros is the energy to envision and build healthy relationships and committed community. Eros moves us into humility.

Erotic power is about integration, connection, and community. Brock tells us that "the paradox of personal power is its relational base. We can only become self-aware and self-accepting through relationships that co-create us and the maintenance of nonharmful environments requires sustained, nurturing relationships. Self-acceptance, as an ongoing, lifelong process, is possible only through our openness to others and their presence."[26] Erotic power invites us to live by heart, in tune with the movements of the Holy Spirit and the world around us.

> This experience of heart enables us to affirm ourselves not at the expense of others, but rather in a way that is life-enhancing to us and others . . . erotic power empowers us all to seek intimacy rather than dependency. It entices us toward openness and self-love and away from the altar of self-sacrifice and self-negation.[27]

A healthy relationship to power builds intimacy, interconnectedness, and mutuality.

There are seasons in our life when growth and survival require that we assume a position of vulnerability. Medical doctors, professors, pastors, and lawyers are professionals who are in a "power-over" relationship with us. We need to be vulnerable in order to receive support, help, and guidance. We trust that these professionals have our best interests at heart and that they are attentive to our needs.[28] The one in the power-over relationship, whether a religious leader or another professional, is responsible for maintaining boundaries and priorities, exercising self-restraint and building trust. In such a professional-client relationship, however, our power still exists. We are exercising our power toward healing, education, and reconciliation by seeking the support and guidance of the expert. We are ultimately responsible for ourselves and must not surrender our voice through compliance or silence. We always have the choice of ending the relationship if a professional acts inappropriately in any way.[29]

Benedict seems to have understood the dynamic of power issues. His *Rule* allocates sufficient time for every monastic to learn to read and write.[30] Time is to be spent in study and intellectual pursuits. Public reading at meals provides nourishment for the soul. He balances this with provision for all to do manual labor. Rank is determined by date of entrance or virtue, not by birthright. Distribution of goods is according to need, with no favoritism.[31] The sick are to be served as Christ, not disdained.[32] RB 58:25 further stipulates that upon profession of the monastic promise, the monastic does not even have power over one's own body. Benedict set up structures to support mutuality and collaboration, warning those with authority to be compassionate and sensitive.

With "living lectio" we deepen in awareness of our God-given power. We are mindful of the ways we can be tempted to use our creative power to manipulate others and control circumstances. We grow in our ability to use our power creatively to empower others.

How is power currently operating in our life? What is the power we exercise in our relationships, personally and professionally? When we are under stress, what forms of toxic behavior tend to emerge? Do we subjugate ourselves to a tyrannical inner voice? What does that inner tyrant look like? How do we discern the seeming chaos in our life? In what ways do we work with it toward new life and new possibilities?

Chapter Six

Benedict's Ladder of Humility Re-considered

here is a wealth to be found in Benedict's Ladder of Humility by probing it through the lens of a feminist approach with some of the important contributions of the social sciences. A helix is cylindrical or a spiral. I want to explore humility as an organic, dynamic helix: always in motion, growing, and returning us to our origins. Seeking contemporary meaning and relevance, I hope to flesh out the *Good News* that liberates and challenges us in our inner journey toward conversion and transformation.

The first step of humility is to utterly flee forgetfulness by keeping the fear of God always before our eyes. We must constantly recall the commandments of God, continually mulling over how hell burns the sinners who despise God. We should guard ourselves

> at all times from sins and vices: of thoughts, tongue, hands, feet, or self-will, but also desires of the flesh. Let each of us take into account that we are constantly observed by God from heaven and our deeds everywhere lie open to the divine gaze and are reported by the angels at every hour . . . (RB 7:10–13).[1]

Benedict's use of the phrase *fear of God* is mostly lost on the current generation. We would much rather ignore God than be "afraid" of God, which is the literal reading. Our distrust of this word may come from negative experiences. Fear is used to control others and extract blind obedience. Too often parents and teachers resort to fear tactics rather than engaging children in meaningful conversation. Also, too many women are afraid of men—and Christianity mostly focuses on masculine images of God—so God is simply one more "man" to be afraid of and to hide from. Power-over images are perpetuated.

In Benedict's era, the understanding of the phrase *fear of God* was that of profound love, respect, and awe.[2] It was the attentiveness of a servant in the presence of a caring master. This mindfulness is grounded in awe, astonishment, and exultation in the Divine Presence. It acknowledges that God is the Creator and we are the created. This opens our hearts to be receptive to God's action in our lives. Benedictine scholar Adalbert de Vogüé sees Benedict's use of the phrase *fear of God* as being *pregnant with love.*[3]

Based on the Hebrew words *torah, yareh,* and *sedeq,* someone who fears God is teachable, a good student, open to new ideas or ways of thinking, is willing to seek and listen, and speaks the truth in seeking justice. Wisdom literature found throughout the Hebrew and Christian Scriptures teaches that the *fear of God* is the beginning of wisdom. Jesus, the incarnation of the Wisdom of God, models for us this healthy, eager willingness to learn, and to be shaped and molded into the image of God.

Benedict reminds us that the beginning of the spiritual journey is remembrance, awareness, and a desire to learn. This is a good portrayal of one who begins to question narrow, exhausted God images. It describes one who is willing to shift from dogma toward spirituality and who begins to break from cultural norms, especially religious cultural norms. The journey moves from a static place to one of life and vibrancy.

Benedict begins his Ladder of Humility with spiritual awakening and a yearning for God. We begin to realize there is something more awaiting us; there is a growing awareness of our walking always in the presence of God. There are early inklings that a revolution is underway, that we haven't known our *truest self* and we hunger to return home. We are divinely lured to move within and the interior world takes on a new importance in our daily lives.

For many women, spiritual awakening opens our awareness of anger and fear dwelling within. We become aware of the ways we have been silenced and denied a voice, and of the ways we have cooperated with our marginalization. We begin to realize that our religious tradition has perpetuated purely masculine God images. The history of our foremothers of the faith has been all but lost, and our theology overshadowed by the theology of our brothers.[4] Women also begin to notice two powerful illusions operating in their lives. One orientation is exultant: I am a powerful, independent woman capable of handling life's journey all by myself. This shows a fierce independence and self-reliance that does not build relationships but tends toward isolation and a need to control. The other pole is equally distorted: I am powerless, I need others to tell me who I am and that I am worthy. I am not sufficient within myself. This shows a dependency on the opinions of others. Both poles, fierce independence and false powerlessness, tend to depend on external structures of authority.

Kegan's helix reveals the necessary journey toward a healthy interdependence, a journey that is more complex than the simple linear. This journey deepens a sense of our authentic power to call forth life and protect it. This means listening to the healthy tension between solitude and community and independence and connection. Spiritual awakening and yearning are divine life pulses of creation and re-creation, continuing and yet ever anew. The helix twists and turns, remains in contact with its origin while progressing in complex growth, and begins ever anew. With the first step of humility, the impetus is remembrance of the source and goal of our life, God.

✠

The second step of humility is not to delight in satisfy-
ing our desires out of love for our own way (RB 7:31).

Benedict's second step addressed the human tendency toward a
desire for control and pursuit of pleasure for pleasure's sake alone.
Benedict called his followers to let go of all intent to fulfill self in
favor of seeking to fulfill God's desire. He understood that setting
aside self enables us to see new perspectives and possibilities. We
are stretched to connect with others.

Many of us struggle to know and then trust our true desires. We
yearn to believe God even cares about our desires, or that our
deepest and truest desires might be God's Will for our lives. This
is deeply connected with our struggles to discover our center and
find our authentic voice.

Women are particularly socialized to ignore personal desires
and to sacrifice self to care for others. A woman may need to

> develop the unfamiliar habit of analyzing every-
> thing in terms of her own self-interest. This requires
> reconnecting with one's ability to sense danger,
> learning to trust one's own opinions, learning to
> evaluate on the basis of how something feels from
> one's own point of view rather than how it looks
> from someone else's. To someone who has been
> treated as if others' needs matter more than her
> own, this is as challenging task.[5]

Pastoral Theologian Brita Gill-Austern points out that

> the equation of love with self-sacrifice, self-denial,
> and self-abnegation in Christian theology is danger-
> ous to women's psychological, spiritual, and physi-
> cal health, and it is contrary to the real aim of
> Christian love.[6]

She continues by pointing out that the tendency for women to define themselves in terms of connectivity and relation gets perverted by our culture into putting the needs of others—especially of men and children first—at the cost of her own personhood. Contemporary cultures tell women that they must sacrifice self and personal needs in order to remain connected and related.[7] Economies and legal systems that keep women financially and socially dependent upon men have reinforced this.

Doctor Jean Baker Miller points out that women have developed a sense that their lives should be guided by the constant need to attune themselves to the wishes, desires, and requirements of others. Often women cannot allow themselves activities that are "only" for themselves. When women have received little real nurturing in their lives, they try to meet this need through care-giving, relieving their own pain by identifying with the pain of others. Not believing deep in their souls that they are truly good, women try to appear good. Due to self-doubt, women seek to please and win the approval of others.

In my work as a spiritual director, I define original sin as *internalized self-hatred*. This has been more helpful and challenging to the people I journey with than any traditional theological definition. Gill-Austern tells us that

> women are motivated toward self-sacrifice by the unholy trinity of self-abnegation, self-doubt, and false guilt which is always knocking on the door of women's lives. Women often behave in self-sacrificial ways because they believe they are less important, less valuable, and less essential than men.[8]

Having the perfect body; thinking like a man; self-sacrifice; attuning self to the wishes and desires of others; and experiences in school and at work where ideas, insights, and experiences have not been taken seriously have reinforced the *internalized self-hatred* that leaves women believing that they are fundamentally flawed.

Self-loathing damages the inner journey and distances us from God. It keeps us from the search because we doubt God would want us near. To the extent that we love ourselves as we are, we are able to truly love God. Theologian Anne Bathurst Gilson tells us that

> God is wrapped up in our *self-loving*. Self-loving is not selfish: it is self-full—of both knowing and loving. Through self-loving, God comes nearer. Self-loving enables us to claim our moral agency, together with one another and God, to seek justice in this world, to stop the eroticized violence, the evil, that is predicated on self-hate, other-hate, God-hate.[9]

Benedict invites his followers to begin the process of interior detachment; to let go of all that possesses us and hinders our ability to hear and respond to God. Although painful, the process of detachment is liberating. We begin to see attitudes, motives, emotional ties, and thoughts that have held us back from a deepened relationship with God and ourselves. Benedict, in the desert tradition, is concerned with all that possesses us: Attachments and compulsions must be recognized in order for healing and liberation to begin. We begin to see hints of *internalized self-hatred* and the ways this has impacted and shaped our life.

Women are presented with a challenge and opportunity for growth. In order to set aside our own will, we must know what our will is. It is an exercise in humility for women to discover, give voice to, and act on our desires. It is necessary to discern between those desires that are God's Will and those that are passing whims, our own selfishness grounded in fear, or a need for control. The journey of discernment reveals many aspects of our self. We are able to gain some self-understanding around the issues, values, and attachments that limit our interior freedom.

The journey of interior detachment teaches us to recognize some of the power dynamics operating in our lives. This includes an awareness of where our power lies, what we do with it, and how we have interacted with the power of others.

Benedict calls his followers to be aware of the tendency toward a strong self-will. This inclination to control life by demanding our own way and to dictate to others how they ought to be living theirs is the belief that we know what is best. Self-will is to break one's covenant relationship with others.

To know our deepest desires is not necessarily to be strong willed. Rather, we can discern how God calls us to fulfill and live out our desires with detachment and interior freedom. We trust that the God who created us with these passions and desires intends to fulfill them. It is not our burden to figure this out, only to trust in the unfolding.

The helix of humility challenges us to live with the paradox and healthy challenges of honoring self and interconnectedness, of bringing a healthy sense of self to community, and growth in interior freedom while honoring the God-created passions and desires within. Remembrance, where we allow the Holy One to reveal our original self, impels us toward growth in humility. In this struggle, we deepen in our love for God. We begin to renegotiate our relationship with God.

☩

The third step of humility is to submit to the superior
in all obedience for love of God (RB 7:34).

Benedict's understanding of obedience was one of action: instant and wholehearted. Monastics were not simply to hear. Obedience meant that the monastic acted upon what was heard. Monastics understood and experienced obedience as movement toward interior freedom.

Obedience was also about discernment.[10] The monastic shared what was on his or her mind and heart with the monastic leader, then let go of any need or determination to get one's own way. Insights were shared with leadership and community, and then decisions were made and accepted.

Benedict's summons to obedience requires trust and calls forth the courage to risk. Will the God who began this journey stay with us each day? Would God abandon us in the midst of pain and challenges? The call is to obedience grounded in freedom. Our *self-within-relationship* does not obey merely to maintain the safety of belonging or to please others. Obedience is thoughtful, prayerful, and actively engaged in the building of community. This obedience does not silence the self; rather it provides the necessary freedom for mature self-discovery.

As we grow in detachment and interior freedom, as we become familiar with our power issues and need for asserting our self-will, we begin to recognize the value of voluntarily allowing another person to have a significant influence in our lives. Discernment with our superior and community moves power issues toward a healthier place in our lives. We increasingly experience the positive strength found in mutual interdependence. Benedict reminds us that our motivation is a healthy one—love of God. We are not handing our power over to the superior in order to abnegate self-responsibility, out of a poor self-image, or because of hero-worship. We unite our gift of power for common purposes. We refine who the voices of authority are in our life and examine how we listen and respond to them. We begin to see a process of transformation in the difficult work of balancing polarities in our lives. As seekers and as Benedictines, we listen deeply to the stirrings of the Holy Spirit in the midst of personally painful tensions existing within the Church today.

Mutuality, deeply valued in many of our homes and monasteries today, is neither about equal power relations nor a reciprocal give and take. Rather mutuality is about sharing power. Mutuality is an ongoing movement. Theologian Carter Heyward speaks of mutuality as a process of relational movement that is held in healthy tension.[11] This is a process of getting unstuck, moving through impasses, of coming into our power together. Calling forth the best in one another, we empower each other to be who we are at our best.

Mutuality is an interrelationship by which we create and liberate one another, redirecting wrong relational power. It requires a commitment to listening with the *ear of our hearts* in such a way that we are willing to be changed by what we have heard. Mutuality also requires a willingness to speak the truth and not evade the quest. Mutuality requires a commitment to stay with one another, even when it is messy or uncomfortable.

Growth in humility and mutuality teaches an appreciation for the hard work of leadership and the qualities needed for effective and empowering leadership. We are part of the empowering process. We are willing to be mentored and shaped by the wisdom of others. Our personal power is committed to this process. As we struggle to follow the lead of leadership in obedience and fellow monastics in mutual obedience, we come to trust the process of leading and following, even leading by our following.

With the helix of humility, we are growing in love for God. We are continually learning who we are and who God is, as opposed to the God we "create." We continue to grow in self-awareness and interior freedom. We are deepening in personal authority and inner strength. The fruit of this journey is healthy connection with others and interdependence.

✠

The fourth step of humility is this: when obedience involves harsh, hostile things or even injustice of some sort, we embrace them patiently with no outcry (RB 7:35).

Benedict knew that monastic life was not easy. The reality is that we are all "under construction": wounded, learning in the midst of our ignorance, fearful, anxious, and frightened. In other words, we are sheep! Imperfect people rub against each other and expose their growing edges. Some of Benedict's wisdom about the realities of community life was learned from his own experience living with a fairly diverse group in his monastery. His monks were from a variety of social and economic classes: slave and free, Roman and barbarian, educated and illiterate.[12] Culture clashes were familiar to him; so was the human tendency to run. Benedict insisted that his followers actively embrace the challenges of the monastic life. He trusted that spiritual maturity and a mature commitment would result.

For many women, naming and confronting the injustice perpetuated against them is more difficult than enduring it. Often confronting injustice results in a shift in relationship. The unknown can be quite fearful until the self is explored and familiar. Familiar pain can feel more comfortable than the risk of an unknown healing process. When we know our strengths, we can converse with our fears.

Conflicts and difficult situations deepen our awareness of personal triggers; those areas where our reactions are out of proportion to the situation. Seeking resolution and reconciliation matures us and strengthens our interior discipline. Benedict calls us to the kind of courageous faith to trust that when we work through a difficult situation, God will be present and *all shall be well.*[13] We trust that God will act toward reconciliation.

As we progress in our growth in humility, we become increasingly disillusioned with our illusions. We gain clearness to see the heart of the conflict. We deepen our freedom to respond by refusing to be hooked by others, and find more creative ways to respond.

As we become more secure, we are less likely to be defensive. We move beyond an instinctual need for self-justification. Pilgrimage toward conversion of heart begins when we are willing to look at the perspective of our adversary—our personal power becomes empowering. A just use of power begins to emerge. Authentic authority is growing from within rather than from somewhere outside one's self. With interior freedom we can avoid impulsive reactions that we later regret. Our self-image is not so dependent upon the opinions and behaviors of others. Through maturing self-awareness and God-awareness, we do not immediately react. Confrontations become conversations toward resolution and relationship building. Our actions in a conflict are based upon prayerful reflection and discernment.

Obedience strengthens and supports the helix of humility. The flexibility and reliability of the helix is revealed, hence we are able to trust the process of interconnectedness and relationship with others. We learn to trust the discernment of our faith community and the people we are committed to, even when it is difficult.

✠

> The fifth step consists in revealing through humble confession to our monastic leader all evil thoughts that enter our heart as well as evil secretly committed (RB 7:44).

Benedict lived before the development of the Sacrament of Reconciliation as we understand it today. He sought to promote a relationship of openness, trust, and discernment between superior and monastic. The superior, chosen by God for wisdom, compassion, and a caring heart, struggled together with the monastic over problems, conflict, and sin.

For many, the word "confession" is a significant trigger, usually around nebulous feelings of guilt that merely serve to reinforce *internalized self-hatred*. Confessing the truth of one's goodness and the truth of where one has been victimized or silenced may be the most difficult words a monastic can share with a superior. Theologian Elizabeth Horst explains that

> traditional religious practices can unintentionally reinforce victim's shame. Someone who lives in constant shame will likely understand religious language and teaching differently from someone who does not. It is very important to understand that the same words will take on different meanings to different people at different times.[14]

In a stance of vulnerability with our superior or spiritual director, we have the opportunity to share the most unwanted parts of our inner process and of ourselves. We can show our truest self to others; that self that we are still discovering and seeking to understand. We choose to accept and believe we are worthy of love and acceptance. Through the process of communal discernment, an integration of interior suffering unfolds. We name and own our addictions, compulsions, and issues. We discover that our deepest suffering is from within as we acknowledge the ways we have perpetuated our own *false self* and then embrace the possibility of resurrection.

We are accountable for our use of power. Are we building community or destroying it? Are we aware of our gift of power and using it, or denying its presence and acting out in other ways? Such conversations also allow us the opportunity to deepen our awareness of how we are using our power and how God might be calling us to use it.

Power enables us to support others in building and sustaining necessary relationships for community, work, and creativity; or we can use it to disrupt and engage in power struggles. We can use our power to contribute to or detract from important relationships. We can support others and ourselves in the monastic observance; we can "show the way" by our words and living example. Power can be effectively focused on the interior journey. It is the power-ful and empower-ing person that has cultivated an interior simplicity and detachment.

The helix of humility impels us to deepen in self-awareness and self-knowledge, significant sources of interior strength. In this stance of growing self-knowledge, we risk trusting others in a stance of vulnerability. This, in turn, builds the bonds that connect us with others and God.

✠

The sixth step occurs when we are content with low
and dishonorable treatment. And regarding all that
is commanded us, we think of ourselves as a bad
and worthless worker (RB 7:49).

Benedict lived in an age of slavery. Only slaves did manual labor in Roman society. Benedict did away with social status and commanded all monastics to share in manual labor as an integral part of the monastic observance. For those monastics that had been used to being served, grumbling probably resulted.

Hopefully, today we understand that all work, no matter what it is, is dignified. We are challenged to continue deepening in detachment, thereby not confusing our worth or place in life by our job title. We are challenged to avoid the trap of thinking too highly of ourselves due to our career successes or sliding into despair when career plans do not materialize as we dreamed. There is a clear gospel call to do justice and to treat one another as Christ. It seems, however, that Benedict is referring more to assigned tasks than to how monastics treat one another.

Benedict reminds us that we are a part of the organic whole and our power is given for the good of the whole. We do not need to be in charge. No task in the monastery is below our dignity or worth. We are not defined by the nature of our work. We are not our work! Our power is realized in our weakness, a deeper awareness of our fragility and utter dependence on God. This is the place where our personal will works with rather than against the movement of the Holy Spirit.

With the helix of humility, there is a forward thrust: Reconciliation with self in our inner emotional and spiritual world impels and sustains reconciliation with others. Detachment toward reputation and status strengthens our interior freedom. Even our shame may be resurrected into joy; a movement away from despair toward hope as there is no obstacle to God's love for us.

✠

> The seventh step of humility is surmounted if we not only confess with our tongue, but also believe with all our heart that we are lower and less honorable than all the rest. Thus declaring with the Prophet: *I am a worm, not human. I am the object of curses and rejection. I was raised up, but now I am humiliated and covered with confusion.* Along the same lines: *It is good for me that you humiliate me, so that I might learn your commandments* (RB 7:51–54).

Now there is a profound interiorizing of the monastic journey. The monastic life comes more from our gut than from our thinking and choices and will. We are deeply aware that we are dependent on God's grace for our monastic observance. We willingly embrace lowliness, a place where we have experienced opportunities for growth.[15] We are also presented with a call to profound self-awareness, so that we come to know ourselves in our deepest humanity: gifts, frailty, and unrealized potential.

Most of us would rather be soaring eagles than lowly worms. Worms are unseen or, at best, barely noticed. Yet our ecosystem is deeply dependent on their presence and vital work. Worms work with what is available. They turn what is "useless" into the soil that sustains life. Worms receive sustenance and strength from their surroundings. They are faithful to their work without drawing attention to themselves. Worms are diverse. There are particular types of worms for particular kinds of tasks. Organic farmers use these different kinds of worms to create the soil necessary for healthy crops.

Benedict developed an earthy *worm theology*. Community is the soil where we toil; we can complain about what we must work with or we can resurrect our allotted "garbage" into the sustenance of life. Flawed families, imperfect colleagues, fellow monastics with an abundance of foibles all become the realm of our worm-activity. Community is hard to tolerate at times, yet from messes emerge the nutrient soil for the work of God's call in our lives. Much that seems messy has an order and purpose to it. A worm theology recognizes the little resurrections of our hard-won growth. Writer Margaret Wheatley states that:

> In chaos theory, strange attractors are the patterns revealed by the order inherent in chaos. A chaotic system wanders wildly, never repeating itself. Each behavior is new and unpredictable. Moment to moment the system is free to experiment. And yet there is a hidden geography to its experimentation. Something unknown calls to its wanderings and the system answers by keeping its explorations within bounds. The attractor calls the system to a certain terrain, to a certain shape.[16]

In the humus of community, and especially when we are fortunate to be in a community that shares a dedication to the faith journey, there is an unseen intelligence to the dynamic of relationship that impels our chaos toward harmony.

Humility invites us to reevaluate what the world may have considered undignified and worthless. The monastic journey is embedded in the local culture and at the same time prophetically critical of it. We are invited to see anew with the eyes, heart, and mind of Christ, and to restore dignity to that which has been deemed worthless. Our strong and mature self does not accept demeaning and marginalizing treatment. Rather we speak liberating truth and do justice, just as worms quietly revolutionize the ecosystem.

This kind of transformation begins within our heart. We choose to see the dignity of worms, even when we do not particularly believe this in our heart. Worms have something to teach us. Life all around us is ready to support us. By discerning the particular tasks God created us for, we can enter into a way of life and work that is best suited to us. When life sends us crushing blows, new opportunities emerge. Worms announce the many resurrections of life; just notice what happens when one is cut in half!

Humility teaches us of our capacity to do evil. We become more deeply aware that the potential for doing what our enemy does— what "wicked" people do—lies within ourselves as well. We develop a capacity to dialogue with those who harm us. We live with a growing sense of awareness of God's profound mercy. We are more aware of the contradictions within ourselves and of the source of our motivations.

The helix of humility reveals that our compassion is experienced at a deeper level. Often we make compassionate choices that may cost us very dearly, but they come from an integrated and wholesome self. Power is grounded deeply in our truest self. We recognize that our power is grounded in being who we really are, as we really are, and as we are called to be. This is a gut-centered humility.

✠

The eighth step of humility is when we do nothing except what is encouraged by the common rule of the monastery and the example of the seasoned members of the community (RB 7:55).

Benedict addressed the need for mutual obedience within the living tradition of the monastic's own monastery.[17] Benedict understood that as the monastic grew in humility, his heart would become one with the heart of the community; authentic unity came from the core of one's being. Benedict had no need for wandering monastics, roaming from house to house, looking for a comfortable place to stay. He condemns this type, called Sarabaites and gyrovagues, early in his Rule.[18] Benedict counters any such tendency by calling his followers to internalize the particular traditions of their community.[19] Yet the healthy dynamic of the helix of humility keeps the community from idolizing its house traditions so that new ideas and possibilities can flow.

The strength that comes from a healthy sense of self and a just use of our God-gifted power allows us the interior freedom to desist from asserting our own will. Our uniqueness as individuals is being woven deeply into the fabric of community. We are increasingly becoming of one heart; our healthy self is part of the whole.

Healthy humility enables communication to move to a more diverse and complex stage. Speech is more authentic and intentional. We speak directly from our heart. We are willing to share the fruit of our prayer and discernment, and are able to let go of this once it has been shared. We are moving into a mature mindfulness and attentiveness with a focused, determined, and mature inner simplicity. As we have become of one heart with our monastic community, our use of power is seasoned and directed by community discernment.

✠

The ninth step of humility comes when we hold back our tongue from speaking and, out of love for silence, do not speak until we are asked a question. Scripture shows that *in much talk, one does not escape sin,* and *the chatterbox does not walk straight on the earth.*

The tenth step of humility consists in not being quick to laugh at the slightest provocation.

The eleventh step of humility is that when we speak
at all, we do so gently and without laughter, humbly
and seriously, with few and careful words. And let
us not be given to shouting (RB 7:56–60).

Benedict does not have a particularly original teaching on
silence.[20] In his previous chapter, he provides his followers with a
simplified explanation of the monastic and desert tradition on
silence.[21] There is a type of progression here. Silence is valued in
itself and we choose to help our community cultivate it. Then we
can grow in a mature sense of humor that moves us into life rather
than away from it. Finally, every movement of our body, every
encounter, and every activity needs to foster a gentle spirit of
silence. Those who honored their yearning for silence and cultivated it learned to say more with fewer words.

Benedict was not interested in the mere absence of words;
rather, he wanted his followers to cultivate an interior silence. This
begins with eliminating vicious, malicious, and sarcastic talk.
Loud, boisterous, and frivolous talk is also avoided. Gentle humor,
however, was found in Benedict's monastery.

Choosing our words before we speak keeps us intentional about
our speech. Benedict wanted his followers to cultivate an interior
serenity, calmness, gentleness, and wisdom; any words spoken
come out of this rich soil. Benedict understood that words reveal
and even betray our heart. He knew that God is encountered in
silence. Cultivating inner silence prepares us for an encounter
with God and helps us to discern the whisperings of God. This
quality of silence comes from a life lived intentionally. We are
attentive and mindful in our daily doings.

A healthy kind of relationship with words and silence comes out
of an integrated and balanced sense of self and a wholesome relationship with power. Words easily reveal poor self-image, bitterness, unresolved anger, or a perverted relationship with power.
Our speech can also reveal a heart of gratitude, joy, and a sense of
adventure.

The helix of humility has drawn the seeker into the depths of a
rich silence. The interior discipline that results from cultivating
comfort with silence deepens wisdom and spiritual maturity.

Silence supports and sustains the interior work where our prophetic call may begin. Any of us called to speak difficult and challenging words of reform or conversion must be grounded in nurturing silence.

Benedict was not seeking to discourage wisdom or the prophetic word. He was concerned with silencing anything that distracts us from God. All who once struggled to find their voices now have the freedom to discern when and where to voice their wisdom. Finding one's voice does not mean we must speak endlessly.

✠

The twelfth step of humility is achieved when our humility is not only in our hearts, but is apparent in our very body to those who see us. That is, whether we are at the Work of God, in the oratory, in the monastery, in the garden, on a journey, in the field, or anywhere at all, whether sitting, walking, or standing, let our head always be bowed and our gaze be fixed on the earth. Constantly aware of our guilt for sins, we should consider ourselves to be already standing before the terrifying judgment of God. We should always repeat in our heart what the publican said in the gospel, our eyes cast downward: *I am a sinner and not worthy to raise my eyes to heaven.* And also with the Prophet: *I am bowed down and totally humbled* (RB 7:62–66).

Just as we think we are reaching the heights of spiritual mysticism, Benedict sends us directly back to the beginning. One of the strengths of the helix is that it never loses touch with its beginnings; the origins are everywhere along the helix. So Benedict reminds us that we "never arrive." One aspect of the monastic promise is *conversatio morum*, meaning fidelity to the monastic way of life; the monastic commits to lifelong learning. This monastic is open to all of life as teacher and cultivates a heart attentive to the teaching moment.

It is good to be in touch with our hunger. When we are not satisfied with what we have accomplished, we strive to be better. We yearn always for God and we cultivate a remembrance of truth. So we remain open to being mentored. We remain always aware of our simple beginnings and we learn from our mistakes. We begin the spiritual journey yet again, now more self-aware. The helix always takes us back again to our origins.

With the fruit of humility, there is a growing congruence between our inner and outer world. Our behavior more closely matches our words; we walk the talk. We are becoming whole. With the helix of humility we are ever growing nearer to our real selves while remembering our spiritual childhood. We return to our beginnings with a greater awareness of our *internalized self-hatred*: the insidiously subtle ways that we cooperate with the *evil one* in undermining our coming home to our truest, most authentic selves.[22]

✠

Therefore, when we have climbed all these steps of humility, we will soon arrive at that *perfect love of God which drives out fear*. We will do this no longer out of fear of hell but out of love for Christ, good habit itself, and a delight in virtue. Once we have been cleansed of vices and sins, Christ will graciously make all this shine forth in us by the power of the Holy Spirit (RB 7:67–70).

In time the spiritual journey will become easier and more joyful. While recognizing the progress we have made, we anticipate with delight the possibilities that lay before us. Due to increasing interior freedom, we are able to anticipate in hope without a need to control how this will be or when it will come to pass. We are now beginning to recognize that we are a partner in the *divine dance*.

With each step of humility, our self grows healthier and freer. Our self becomes a self we can let go of without personal degradation or destruction. With each step of humility we grow more aware of our power and become freer to make right use of it. As we deepen in humility, God-images change and expand. With the strength that comes from living from our God-created truest selves and a healthy expression of power, idols come crashing down and a new awareness of who God is emerges.

As we deepen in humility, we have the strength to allow God to reveal Divine Self rather than our creating boxes that we "require" God to dwell in. Theologian Anne Bathurst Gilson speaks of this maturing God-image:

> God is radically immanent. . . . God moves and is moved, changes and is changed, touches and is touched. . . . God is a God who is moved, changed, and touched into an *ongoing solidarity* in which we move, change, and touch while standing *with* one another. Being with God in solidarity means that God does not walk away from relation or from conflict. We are all in it together, always.[23]

Growth in humility is a movement toward the *anawim*, those truly despised, vulnerable, and forgotten that are near to God's heart.[24] This movement is intentional, made by our daily choices. Drawing close to the anawim brings about unity, oneness, and wholeness. Jesus calls us closer to the anawim; the divine paradox is that the weakest and despised are the very strength of the helix.

The anawim may also be those disdained parts of ourselves, the internalized self-hatred that we struggle to face, to extend compassion toward, and allow the Holy Spirit to heal. When we reach out to the anawim, sharing our voice and power with them, we are healing that part of ourselves that we despise.

As we deepen our capacity for self-reflection and mature in self-awareness, we become increasingly attentive to God, seeking

> ongoing, vital, incarnate relationships with thinking, feeling, choosing, passionate people who, under the inspiration of the Spirit within, co-create their lives day by day. To enact one's belief that religion is essentially a vital relationship with the Holy One is to live a profoundly creative spiritual life.[25]

Humility is love incarnate. Humility is the journey to *realized resurrection*. In humility, we have a healthy, mature relationship with God.

"Living lectio" asks us to ponder the ways this discussion of humility has disturbed us and possibly angered us. How were our strongly held beliefs disrupted? How has it relieved us? What are we invited to?

What helps us honestly and quietly embrace the person we truly are before God? In what ways do we resist coming home to ourselves and our communities or families? How do we honor the strengths and limitations God has gifted us with? What are some of the snares we are liable to fall into that reinforce our public persona and diminish our truest self? What messages—subtle, insidious, and devious—reinforce our sense of internalized self-hatred and self-loathing? What are we listening to?

How do we draw close to God? What do we do when we become aware of hindrances to deepening intimacy with God? How do we express our personal power and powerfulness? In what ways do we empower others? What are we doing with our "distorted exhaltations"?

What hooks—fears, beliefs, distorted self-images—keep us attached to things, people, or ideas? What do we need to do to move toward internal freedom?

Which persons make up our community of committed interdependence? Do we resist the connectedness of community or receive it? What do we do with our seasons of resistance? Will we risk challenging others in our community toward growth?

To what—people, institutions, theologics, and ideologies—do we grant authority in our life? How do we responsibly relate to those authorities: in a thinking, pondering, reflecting, and prayerful manner?

How are compassion, grace, and mercy seasoning our approach to life? How do we effect reconciliation? How do we cultivate awareness of our powerfulness? How do we balance our personal power and authority with the power and authority of our colleagues?

Chapter Seven

Lenten Considerations

Saint Benedict believed that the monastic observance is a *continuous Lent: at all times the lifestyle of a monastic ought to have a Lenten quality.*[1] Lent was a season of joy and celebration for Benedict. He admonished his followers to fulfill their Lenten observance *with the joy of the Holy Spirit.* Our observance is in a ready and spontaneous spirit of joyful love.

Benedict was refreshingly gentle with his followers, calling for a focused purity of observance. He was concerned that our Lenten journey should come from the heart and not merely external observances. Benedict tells us to *deny our body some food, some drink, some sleep, some chatter, some joking, and let us await Holy Easter with the joy of spiritual desire.*[2] Benedict believed that Lent led to a deepened spiritual maturity. Benedictine spirituality is earthy, embodied, and genuine; our Lent must be the same. We must be authentic in our pilgrimage through Lent, the Triduum and resurrection.[3]

Asceticism

Most of my adult life I wrestled with a sense of inadequacy at observing the call to practices of asceticism. There were periodic successes but I mostly failed at fasting and self-denial. I was making attempts, with the best of intentions, on my own strength. Rather than listening for God's guidance, I defined asceticism and then attempted to follow my program. Failure only fed the internalized messages of worthlessness. With all my well-intentioned efforts, I did not come to know God more intimately.

I finally came to the realization that God hands us our asceticism through the normal circumstances of everyday life. We only need to be attentive to these opportunities. For many of us, asceticism might include hours spent helping children do their homework, taking time to be present to aging parents or someone hurting, and attending and contributing to countless meetings. Speaking kindly when we'd rather speak a sharp word, speaking honest words of affirmation to others, and making healthy eating and exercise choices are all examples of ways we are called to an asceticism that is God-directed and opens our heart toward the Divine.

Our culture tends toward an ambiguous relationship with asceticism, believing that it is only something for "holy" people, that it is too difficult to sustain, or even that it is irrelevant to our daily life. Some people tend toward the other extreme, confusing self-starvation (anorexia), self-denigration, and other self-defeating attitudes and acts with an authentic asceticism. This serves only to move us away from God. It reinforces a low self-image, diminishes any sense of self-worth, and supports images of a vengeful, wrath-filled God. We then miss out on the sense of God's gentle loving presence.

With authentic asceticism, God respectfully awakens us to our attitudes, motives, passions, desires, and lifestyle. This requires prayerful discernment around where the Image of Christ is expressed and dwells in our life. This also entails the recognition of what is not of Christ. Asceticism is a way of letting go of all that burdens and hinders our growing close to Jesus.

Irritations are an opportunity for ascetic observance and deepening self-awareness. When we are irritated, we have an opportunity to listen within and learn what the dynamic is and how we are being called to let something go. Each person who comes into our midst is an opportunity for asceticism: to literally see and honor the Christ in them, to exercise patience, to stop and simply notice them, and to look into their eyes with love.

Meetings are an opportunity for ascetical practice. Most of us have known days defined by scheduled and unscheduled meetings. Our asceticism could include carefully preparing in advance the materials needed to thoughtfully participate—doing so reflectively and prayerfully. We then commit to being fully present, mentally and emotionally. We share in the responsibility for the quality and dynamic of the meeting, and constructively participate without dominating or controlling the process or end results.

An authentic asceticism exposes our interior attachments, addictions, compulsions, and dependencies. This asceticism also gives us the strength to face our *little idols* and let go of them. Authentic asceticism does not draw attention to us, rather it consists of the small choices we make. Playing or praying when we feel compelled to work; stepping away from our busyness to be with God in the silence and solitude. These choices can be more irritating and inconvenient than the medieval hair shirt! An authentic asceticism challenges us to live in vulnerability and to courageously reveal ourselves to our family, significant friends, and community.

Living lectio invites us to deepen in awareness of the asceticism already placed in our lives. How do we listen? Respond? How do we discern what are authentic asceticism to live through as opposed to life situations we are called to change? How does our asceticism affirm our humanity, connect us with others, and deepen our compassion and awareness? What can we do when our only natural response is hardness of heart?

Fasting and Detachment

Benedict's Rule presumes that the monastic is struggling to live a disciplined life. Fasting went above and beyond the expectations. Benedictine scholar Terrence Kardong tells us that for a monastic to love fasting means that it is now internalized and an integral part of the monastics daily life.[4] For Benedict, fasting supported the internal discipline, which in turn facilitated detachment, which then led to purity of heart.

We would be wise to integrate a positive experience of fasting into the fabric of our spirituality. Fasting from all foods or certain types of foods can help us cultivate inner freedom and interior discipline. The focus is rightly on seeking God, not abstaining from something. Another form of fasting is also helpful: fasting from *my* agenda, *my* church politics, *my* opinions, *my* whatever. Then fasting moves us *toward* another person's worldview and life experience. This is Benedict's fast: no murmuring, grumbling, or complaining! It is the fast of speaking gently and respectfully, straight from our heart. The fruit of the monastic fast is revealed in our deepened patience, empathy, and compassion.

Fasting often reveals much about ourselves: our struggles, values, and endearments. Fasting enables us to be more self-aware and Spirit aware. We are not so burdened with ourselves, with all our fears and compulsions, addictions and agendas. Fasting quiets our interior noise and disorderly inclinations. Our inner world becomes more attentive and alert to the movements of God's Spirit.

A primary goal of the interior journey and of our monastic practices is detachment, which leads toward interior freedom, that place where we are free of everything that disrupts and hampers our relationship to God. Our goal is a life of *abundant simplicity*. Detachment allows for greater direct experience of the Divine Presence as we are attached to fewer distractions. It provides the space for *heart knowledge,* where we come to know our truest self. This is a gut experience of God.

An authentic monastic fast moves us into detachment as we step away from what possesses our heart, mind, and gut. Detachment is that place where blockages are being exposed and removed—all that keeps us from God. This is the movement toward interior freedom. Detachment frees our heart of the burden of all our certitudes and self-righteous attitudes, causing a reordering of our priorities.

With detachment, we work to remove all possible obstacles to a deepening relationship with God. Obstacles take many forms. We could be living with an internalized tyrant who drives us to overachievement, who brings out all the legalistic "shoulds" and "oughts." We may be unaware of our most-favored attachments, such as our career, or our expectations of how God will act, behave, or respond. We could be unaware of our idolatry: those God-images that say, "God is just like this, never like that" in an unconscious attempt to control God. We could be living with a stubborn determination to get our own way.

Subtle messages of "life should be easy" or "life is always hard" can block growth in our relationships with one another and with God. Any thoughts that block us or distract us from our pursuit of God need discernment and healing. Emotional bondage can complicate our inner journey. This can include resentment, bitterness, and unforgiveness. Our fear, anxiety, and anger can keep us from cultivating an open and receptive heart. Enmeshment in other people's lives may be very tempting, but it distracts us from our own difficult interior work. Unfortunately, other people's problems and challenges become fascinating and lure our attention away from our own interior work.

With the cultivation of interior discipline and detachment, our attachments, addictions, and compulsions become reconciled. Less possesses us. Feelings are acknowledged and listened to for their wisdom, but also subjected to the discipline of our heart's goal to seek God. Simplicity of emotion nurtures our focus on God and deepens our intimacy with the Divine. Simplicity of emotion nurtures our interior strength and balanced wholeness.

Cultivating detachment requires courage and determination as suffering often accompanies this process. Suffering has some of its roots in attachment to attitudes, thoughts, and desires. Suffering remains until our heart lets go. Suffering can be the avenue toward freedom, maturity, and humility. Compassion grows.

Living lectio entices us to pay attention to our growth, or lack of growth, in detachment. In what ways are we increasingly filled with joy as we let go? In what ways are we coming to enjoy the unexpected surprises of the spiritual journey? Do we notice our image of God shifting? Are we increasingly comfortable as God is revealed to us as something Other than what we wish for or expect?

Evidence of Detachment

Detachment is *really real*. There is evidence that can be observed and experienced by those around us when we deepen in the interior discipline of detachment. Our growth in detachment is revealed when judgmental and critical attitudes begin to soften. We may see a bit of ourselves reflected in another person's behavior. Instead of reacting with irritation and sharp words, we hold our tongue. We become more tolerant of our own weaknesses and the habits of others as we grow in compassion. We work constructively with our passions and desires. We become far more tolerant of the habits of others and their ways of being, and our irritation level drops.

Detachment fosters a greater understanding of our own true humanity. As we become aware of the ways we might be disrupting community and family, we begin to make changes for the benefit of others. We keep conversations quiet and save our more boisterous fun for appropriate times and places. Our self-awareness and sensitivity to the environment deepens. We quietly clean up after others, we take a little extra time to care for public space, and we contribute joyously to group work teams. As a tender, vulnerable heart is cultivated, an inner calm and serenity emerges.

Detachment deepens our capacity for listening, especially to those things that are difficult for us to hear. Our relationships are no longer possessive and controlling. We notice the tendencies toward projection onto others. We are no longer hemmed in by concern about our reputation or the opinions of others. Instead we focus on discerning God's desires and Will for us.

Inner Freedom

Inner freedom allows us to be more responsive, in a healthy and helpful way, to the needs of those around us. Our response is not based on the personal need: to be needed by others and to control our environment. Rather, we are graced with a capacity to listen to the leading of the Holy Spirit and make discerning choices that balance our needs with the needs of others.

Inner freedom means we are able to live with possessions without being possessed by them or driven to have them. We hold these possessions lightly and use them freely. We are stewards of these goods; they do not belong to us.

Inner freedom is nurtured and supported through self-care. This includes allocating time for lectio and deepening our comfort for silence and for listening. Balancing work and leisure time with solitude, family, and community is foundational. Faithfulness to prayer keeps us focused; leisure time keeps us energized and restores vision. Detachment is our work as we make our choices daily. Detachment is also God's work of luring us closer to one another and the Holy Other.

Listen With the Ear of Your Heart

Benedict calls each of his followers to *listen with the ear of our hearts*. He began his Rule with: *listen to my instructions, turning to them with the ear of your heart. This is advice from one who loves you; welcome it, and faithfully put it into practice.*[5] Heart listening is active, and an interior response is expected. For Benedict, the hearing is demonstrated in the active response. To merely talk about something heard, to ruminate with friends on a word received from the Holy Spirit without acting on this received word is to not listen with the ear of our heart, it is merely to be entertained by the Divine.

Deep listening comes from a discerning stance that involves Scripture, the Rule, and our extended community. We must be willing to listen and continually willing to learn. Listening with the ear of our hearts is honest and communal. It is not an invitation to do our own thing, just "me and God." Lent is a special season of listening.[6] Our monastic observance prepares our hearts and minds for this deep kind of listening.

Listening with the ear of our hearts involves our body, heart, and intellect. Our intuition and bodily sensations tell us if something is of God when we are listening from our grounded and centered being. This is complex listening that requires us to open our heart to the many voices God has placed in our life. It is vital that this include those we tend to dismiss or disdain. When the poor, silenced, marginalized, and forgotten speak, are we willing to listen in a compassionate and responsive stance? When we listen with our heart, their message shapes our prayer, choices, and lifestyle. God has given each of us internal signals for when we are listening well. It is *Divine Risk-taking* to trust that the inner stirrings resulting from our listening, that have been properly discerned with a wise elder, are acted upon in faith. Do we run away from that which entices and lures us?

Why does Benedict want us to listen with the ear of our hearts? Because this churns and sifts and prepares our heart for the presence of the Holy One. This depth of listening moves us out of ourselves and into the heart of God, where we can hear the whisperings of God where once we were deaf. Here we become one with the mystical Body of Christ and the Communion of Saints, as our heart touches theirs. It is at the level of our hearts that we are shaped and formed into true followers of Christ. Our call is to an interior and authentic spiritual journey, and not mere outward behaviors.

Benedict understood that quality listening was an ascetical practice. Long fasts, night vigils, and self-denial all mean nothing if our heart remains cold and rigid, bound by fear and anxiety, deaf to words and people that make us uncomfortable. This is a Lenten journey that involves dying to our own agenda and interior voices. We die to our presuppositions about how life is supposed to be and who God is supposed to be, and are stretched beyond our comfort zone.

Lent is the season of deep and prayerful listening. Our intense observance helps prepare our hearts and minds for the kind of listening that evokes deep changes from within. With Lenten listening, we die to our false self, anxieties, and fears and rise to new perspectives, possibilities, and miracles. The unknown elements, the blocks and blind-spots, are transformed with new vision and hope.

Are we prepared for this encounter? Will we risk the deep and basic listening Benedict calls us to? Are we prepared for a listening that is formative and prophetic and life changing? Living lectio invites us to risk encountering the Lenten seasons of our life.

That Our Joy May Be Full!

A wise elder once told me that joy is the identifying mark of a spiritually mature person. Since my encounter with Benedictine spirituality and the monastic way of life, this piece of wisdom has taken on new and profound meaning for me. I have come to discover the immense joy of the journey as the layers of all that keeps me from the Holy One are peeled away. Joy, even in the midst of difficult times, has become my source of strength and grounding.

We yearn for deeper union with God. As we mature in the monastic way, we become increasingly sensitive to our innate desire for God. We are increasingly frustrated with the blocks and hindrances—the very gulf—between God and ourselves. We yearn to find our truest selves: selves that we do not fully know, yet whose potential we have glimpsed. We begin to see the shadow of possibilities and hints of what God might want for us. We hear and attempt to respond to a call to come home.

Joy is the disposition that emerges abundantly as we deepen in unity with God. We come to delight in the unexpected surprises God sends our way. We come to anticipate and appreciate the broad vision God would have us risk. Having tasted God's inheritance for us, we develop exuberance for the things and ways of God. Our disposition increasingly becomes one of great delight and profound satisfaction, which is Benedict's abiding peace. We start to view life through a lens of abundance rather than scarcity.

In his Rule, Benedict tells us that as *we progress in this way of life and in faith, we shall run on the path of God's commandments, our hearts overflowing with the inexpressible delight of love.*[7] To the extent that we dwell in joy, we know Christ. Joy is internalizing the resurrection. Our monastic observance helps us shed everything that keep us from joy. Lenten observance has its means and its goal in mature joy. And for Benedict, zeal becomes the impetus or motivator toward joy: *So there is a good zeal that separates us from evil and leads to God and everlasting life. Thus we should practice this zeal with the warmest love.*[8]

What keeps us from joy? What keeps us from entering in and basking fully, even scandalously, in the deep and limitless joy of God? What are we holding on to unnecessarily? Why do we observe Lent? **That our joy may be full!**

Chapter Eight

Holy Week Pilgrimage

P alm Sunday and Holy Week, culminating in the Triduum and Easter Resurrection, are the sacred pilgrimage of the Christian way of life. With Holy Week, we journey with Jesus and his followers through anticipation and celebration, friendship and betrayal, resistance to the Empire, crucifixion and death. We dwell in grief and despair to be surprised into life again with the resurrection.

Each year we are invited to make this sacred journey together, living the story again. We are invited to see ourselves among Jesus' friends and companions, busy about daily life, yet knowing something is in the air, an anticipation and quiet dread. We see ourselves among the religious leaders and the Roman soldiers occupying the Holy Land: wanting to get rid of a nuisance. We are among the outcast and discouraged—our hearts filled with pain and heaviness and hopelessness—who have not yet heard the Good News.

On the sacred pilgrimage, we bring our own story, with all its known and unknown facets, to the *Jesus-event* of Holy Week. With Jesus, we live with and through our desires, passions, and pain.

With Jesus, we move forward through the Agony in the Garden of Gethsemane and the Crucifixion into Resurrection. Holy Week does not permit us to dwell stuck in any one place, but beckons us forth to the fullness of resurrection; this call requires movement from us. Holy Week allows us each year to incarnate our own sacred story by unpacking and discovering which parts of us are captive and to discern where God yearns to lead us into freedom.

With Palm Sunday, we are invited to join the *anawim celebration*. Jesus enters Jerusalem in a sea and swirl of the anawim: those people whose sole hope for protection is in the One who has come to show us a new way. We are again reminded that joy can be our natural way of life. The Spirit breathes joy into our hearts, the very core of our being, if we are only willing to join in the dance.

On Palm Sunday we celebrate God's presence in our midst, setting aside pain and stress, worry and fear for the moment. Yet celebration can stir up turmoil. Although freedom is luring us to let go of hindrances to God, we may not feel ready to encounter a big and gracious God. Perhaps our family is not be comfortable with the new, free, and liberated person we are becoming.

With Holy Week, we continue our faithfulness to our religious observance; we practice *Holy Monotony*.[1] Many of our religious practices and observances can seem routine, ordinary, even boring; one more session of meditation, pulling ourselves away from work to pray the Liturgy of the Hours, faithfulness to lectio when work and other responsibilities are calling. We faithfully commit to regularly visiting that sacred space we have created in our homes where we meet with the Holy One. At a deeper level, the Holy Spirit is moving and healing and teaching us from this deep inner core of our being. Holy Monotony grounds us in joy. We live into Holy Week with an expectant heart that *this* time things might be different. . . . But how?

With Jesus' followers, we enter Holy Week unaware of the journey that lies before us. We begin preparations for Passover, now called Holy Thursday by Christians, and look forward to time with comfortable friends and family. This is a *Feast of Freedom*; we are invited to step out of our bondage and celebrate the freedom Jesus has shown us. Prayerful discernment shows us this path toward greater liberation, which is built on healthy interdependent relationships.

Entering Passover celebrations, we begin to see that something is altered and new. We realize that our circle of friends has expanded to include many that we have been taught to open our hearts to and love—because of the One from Nazareth. The meal itself takes on new and nuanced meaning for us.

We pilgrimage with Jesus to the Garden of Gethsemane. He accompanies us as we agonize over betrayal, broken trust, and disloyal friends. This is where we bring our pain, anger, and angst. Here also we confront the ways that *we* have been the betrayer, the disloyal friend, the one who has broken the trust of others. We remain in Gethsemane until there is resolution; we ought not to attempt to depart too soon. Yet we must not get stuck in the Garden ruminating on our pain and forgetting that God's goal is resurrection.[2]

In our agonizing with the *Awesome Silence* of God, Gethsemane requires that we reexamine our images of God. Gethsemane strips us of self-delusion and we are forced to face the atheism lurking deep in our heart. Gethsemane moves us into the realm of injustice we have not deserved and suffering that seems meaningless and for reasons we do not understand.

In the Garden of Gethsemane, we are confronted with our pain and anguish. We are called to let go of our idols and attachments, and stand naked before our God. Here we are invited to sit expectantly in the wilderness of freedom and possibilities, allowing hope to arise from within. This Garden honors the truth of the many gardens in our life's journey.

Then we are taken before the Sanhedrin: our own peers, colleagues, family and friends, and faith community. Our beliefs, theologies, agendas, and issues may be called into question. The once-solid ground we stood confidently on is shaken and unsure. Some of their questions and accusations sting with the depth of truth. We must wrestle with our choices, allegiances, and beliefs. Do they hold firm before the *One Who Is Truth, Justice,* and *Life Itself*? Have we lived authentically, according to our profession of faith? Is there enough evidence to convict us?

Then comes Good Friday, the day of crucifixion. We experience the crushing, noisy crowd; we are struck by pungent odors. Harshness, cruelty, and division fill the air. Anger, anguish, despair, and triumph hits us from every angle. As followers of Christ, we are called to carry the Cross with Simon of Cyrene. We bear the *cosmic burden* of an uncertain future and wonder: how trustworthy and deep is the Holy One's compassion?

As Followers of the Way, we want to cling to Jesus; yet we are afraid to be seen with him. We journey on the edge of the crowd, slowly working our way out of the city walls and on to the *Place of the Skull*. Our hearts are pierced with each blow of hammer on nail. Our despair seems overwhelming. We are reassured by a community of people who love Christ: Mary of Nazareth, Mary the wife of Clopas, Mary Magdalene, Mary the mother of James and Joseph, and the mother of the sons of Zebedee, along with the disciple whom Jesus loved. Each of them are faithfully standing at the foot of the Cross. Then we are overwhelmed by the feeling of abandonment as we hear the last breath of Jesus depart. We ask why and want to scream at the insanity! The words of Saint William of Thierry capture the truth of the moment: *Jesus' crucifixion is sheer holy madness.*

On Good Friday, 1979, Archbishop Oscar Romero of El Salvador told his listeners:

> God is not failing us when we don't feel the Holy Presence.

> Let's not say: God doesn't do what I pray for so much, and therefore I don't pray anymore.

> God exists, and exists even more, the farther you feel from God.

> God is closer to you when you think God is farther away and doesn't hear you.

> When you feel the anguished desire for God to come near because you don't feel God present, then God is very close to your anguish.

When are we going to understand that God not only gives happiness but also tests our faithfulness in moments of affliction?

It is then that prayer and religion has most merit: when one is faithful in spite of not feeling the Lord's presence.

Let us learn from that cry of Christ that God is always our Father and never forsakes us, and that we are closer to God than we think.[3]

On Holy Saturday, we are invited to wait at the tomb. We are not certain why we are there, but acknowledge the inner pull. We wait with expectant hope, the despair of not knowing, or a safe "wait and see" attitude. Here we are confronted with emptiness. God does not seem to be present and our aloneness is therefore vivid. We can try to fill up this space with something other than God, or we can courageously and prayerfully wait in a contemplative stance with great hope. Holy Saturday lays bare what has been hidden: hopes, aspirations, dreams, and desires. Our fears, insecurities, and anxieties are also revealed. With Holy Saturday the seeds lay germinating, waiting the appointed time of breaking forth. Our patience may be stretched to nearly breaking; we may be sorely tempted to fill that empty, hollow space with something other than the Holy One.

Together with Jesus' followers, we are invited to journey into resurrection. Many of us fear the resurrection, often without realizing it. We can focus so much on the crucifixion of Good Friday that we never move through Holy Saturday and into the bursting forth of Easter Sunday. We can give lip service to being resurrection people while our lives are stuck in the fear and anxiety of Gethsemane or the crucifixion. Why are we called to put faith in Christ-crucified? Because of the resurrection! Resurrection is a *power event*. Power, indeed, to bring to life all that we thought lost and hopeless. Power to gift us with new vision and new possibilities. Power to breathe life into places where despair, emptiness, and a void once existed.

Resurrection involves risk. Change involves risk. Resurrection means handing power and control over to God, trusting God in the process. Resurrection means stretching our heart to hold onto the *Resurrection event,* with all its repercussions. In resurrection we let go of a *spirituality of scarcity* and take on God's *spirituality of abundance.* With a resurrection attitude, we see God's gracious and providential care for each of us.

Easter Sunday confronts us with some hard questions: Have we grown comfortable with lifelessness? Have we grown so accustomed to pain that we don't want to let go? Will we let God grow us a big, huge, passionate, opulent heart? We are invited to bring our despair and lifelessness, wants and burdens, attachments and confusions—our whatever—to the place of resurrection. There we risk allowing them to be transformed as God sees fit. With Mary Magdalene, we too are invited to be the *First Witness* to those God has placed in our lives in order that they receive the gift of Jesus' Good News.

What will you bring to Holy Week? What burden, conflict, pain will you hand over to Jesus? Will you expand your hearts to be more intentionally inclusive of those you would rather not sit with? How will you embrace Resurrection in your life? Will you accept the Resurrection gift of utter joy and complete freedom?

Chapter Nine

Hospitality and the Prophetic

Benedictines deeply value hospitality, seeking to literally *receive all as Christ*. Many who have experienced Benedictine hospitality have pondered this experience, deepening their own expression of hospitality toward others and the world. Some have embraced Benedictine ways as oblates and associates.

Benedictines have instinctively understood the work of hospitality as extending mercy and offering reconciliation that they have experienced from God.[1] At times, this hospitality has a prophetic element; prophetic meaning those momentary, utterly transforming encounters with the Divine. We certainly have a long tradition of receiving the prophetic in our midst; hopefully we receive and engage this gift graciously.

In my experience of offering hospitality in our monastery and retreat house, I have experienced a lively, deep, and abiding conversation between our life of hospitality and the prophetic.

This experience has caused me to reflect on the ways monastic life and expressions of Benedictine spirituality in our homes and at work might best create an environment of hospitality that is welcoming to the prophetic.

Hospitality in the Rule of Benedict

✠

All guests who arrive should be received as Christ, who will say: *I was a stranger and you took me in.* Proper respect should be shown to all. As soon as a guest is announced, the monastic leader and community members should hurry to meet the guest with every mark of love. First they should pray together and then be united of peace. The kiss of peace should not be given unless prayer has come first. The greeting itself ought to manifest complete humility toward guests who are arriving or departing: By an inclination of the head or by a complete prostration on the ground, one must adore Christ in them, who is the One received. When they have been received, the guests should be led to prayer, and afterward the monastic leader or one appointed should sit with them. Let the Divine Law be read to the guest for edification, and after that the guest should be shown every sort of kindness. The monastic leader should break the fast on behalf of the guest. The monastic leader should pour water on the hands of the guests. The monastic leader as well as the whole congregation should wash the feet of all guests. When they have been washed, let them pray this verse: *We have received, O God, your mercy in the midst of your temple.* The greatest care should be exhibited in the reception of the poor and pilgrims, for Christ is more especially received in them; for the very fear of the rich wins them respect. The kitchen of the monastic leader and the guests ought to be separate so that the guests, who are never in short supply in the monastery and who tend to arrive at odd hours, will not disturb the community. A monastic whose soul the fear of God possesses should be assigned to the guest quarters. A sufficient number of beds should be made up there. Wise people should manage the house of God. If one meets or sees guests, greet them humbly. The monastic should ask for a blessing and then move on (RB 53).

Benedictine scholar Terrence Kardong points out that Benedict's use of "receive" is closely connected to the "suscipe" or reception of monastic profession. He states that the monastic is "received" at profession so that he can then "receive" others in hospitality."[2] As the monastic gives full mind, heart, body, and spirit to the monastic community and God, so we are called to give to all in hospitality.

The guidelines Benedict gives in his Rule concerning daily life in the monastery are meant to protect the communal monastic observance in order to support, nurture, and preserve the interior spiritual quest. He wanted guests to be received *as Christ* without serious disruption to the community. Ritual prayers and blessings are said in order to discern the heart of the guest. In this way the Living Word within the guest is received by the monastic but any influence of the Evil One is exposed.

Benedict is concerned that the monastic who serves guests recognizes that guests may be vulnerable and basically powerless. Benedict wants all guests treated with gentleness and graciousness, with a special concern for the poor, who only have Christ to protect them.

✠

A monastic from a distant region may arrive for a visit and wish to live in the monastery as a guest. If the monastic is satisfied with the local customs that

> are found there and does not trouble the monastery with excessive demands, the monastic should be allowed to stay as long as they like. If the monastic points out some shortcoming calmly and with loving humility, the monastic leader should consider the matter carefully. Indeed, God may have sent the monastic for that very purpose (RB 61:1–4).

Benedict balances loyalty to monastic observance with the receiving of Christ in the guest. The porter and the monastic leader greet guests warmly, who are then invited into the rhythm of the community's search for God.

Benedict was open to the possibility that the guest may bring with them a prophetic word or insight. He wants us open and receptive to the possibilities of learning. It is also important that we discern messages given in a contemplative stance. This is the monastic commitment to ongoing conversion of life.

✠

> A wise monastic should be stationed at the gate of the monastery. This wise elder should know how to listen to people and also how to speak to them. . . . As soon as anyone knocks or a poor person cries out, respond with "Thanks be to God!" or "Bless me!" Filled with the gentleness of the God-fearer, the monastic must quickly respond in the warmth of charity (RB 66:1–4).

The porter of the monastery is the first face of hospitality. With gentleness and patience, the porter listens to needs and responds appropriately.

It is appropriate and valuable to protect what influences us. Yet we must be open to the God-encounters that come to us in disguise. At the same time we are called to continually cultivate the attentiveness and self-awareness that guards us against hurtful or disruptive influences. As we anticipate Christ's return, so we welcome signs of Christ in our guests.

Hospitality

Have you ever encountered a person or a special place that left you feeling reenergized? Feeling particularly loved? Feeling particularly alive? Restored your hope? Restored your inner vision and sense of purpose in life? This is the place of hospitality.

Hospitality is an attitude of open receptivity toward the persons and events that gift our lives. True hospitality is generous and cherishing and implies the ability to see God in each person. *Hospes*, meaning both guest and host, is a two-way encounter that implies mutuality and sincere graciousness. True hospitality grows out of our own experiences of vulnerability and our awareness of the dignity and sacredness of all of life. Hospitality is rooted in our heart and centered in peace. It is not a superficial, but rather a gut-felt, spiritual encounter. Benedict admonishes us to hurry and greet our guests *with every mark of love* and *pray together and then be united in peace* (RB 53:3–4).

Hospitality lived out in openness to the fullness of life, of humanity, and of human mystery opens us to the possibility of encountering divine mystery. Risking openness to the presence of the divine and especially to the unexpected cultivates the *listening heart* needed to understand the gift and presence of the prophetic in our midst.

Hospitality is related to our experience of the Divine Office. In the Liturgy of the Hours, we receive the hospitality of God: through our chanting of the Divine Word and through our reception of one another. We bring our personal stories and struggles along with the struggles and pain of contemporary society, entering prayerfully into the text. My monastery has developed its Office and ordo to reflect our lived story and our shared values. We pray in inclusive language with expanded God imagery. Our readings for the Evening Office are from the writings of people we do not ordinarily hear: women, men who are willing to risk their positions of privilege, and people of non-dominant cultures. Each proclaims the gospel in their lives and words.

Jesus, as a member of Jewish culture that deeply valued hospitality, challenged his followers to stretch their understanding and practice of inclusivity. For Jesus, hospitality begins with an interior stance or attitude toward life that sees those who are marginalized and oppressed as gifts from God, not burdens. Benedict aimed for hospitality that was grounded in an awareness of the divine presence everywhere.

Our capacity to extend hospitality toward strangers and guests is profoundly related to the quality of relationships within our monastic community. The place where we begin to learn the work and spirit of hospitality is with our place of first life commitment: families, faith community, or religious community. Monastic guests seek a peaceful, safe, and prayerful environment. Such an environment is a result of hard work by community members who are continually building relationships on honesty and trust.

Benedict was concerned about hospitality within his community. In his attention to the details of community living, especially in his Prologue and in RB 72, we see Benedict attending to the quality of community life that was to be the foundation of hospitality extended toward guests. Christ was first to be honored in fellow community members.

Community and family life are a complex and delicate web of relationships that are a testing ground for one's strength of character, spirit of charity, and depth of commitment. These community relationships require us to practice self-care and remain deeply committed to our growth. It is from this well of love that we are able to show the way of growth to others. Opportunities for growth in self-awareness await us in the ordinary daily life of community and family, as we embrace our monastic promise through family commitments, and in our encounter with guests. The cost of refusing these opportunities to let the mundane and ordinary teach us is that we risk expending great energies in resisting these occasions for growth.

My own community is deeply committed to the work of individual self-growth and to building relationships with each other. This commitment to our communal journey is the foundation for our work of hospitality. These relationships make our individual and corporate work of discernment possible. The strength of these relationships empowers us to discern our response to the prophetic voice within our community and that of our guests.

The environment of Benedictine hospitality seeks to be safe, quiet, reflective, and prayerful. The monastic promise keeps us from running from difficulties. Instead these difficulties become the place where compassion, empathy, and wisdom are cultivated. A contemplative stance nurtures those who come into our lives.

The process of providing an atmosphere of hospitality and of journeying with the prophetic helps to prepare our hearts to receive an important word. We usually do not recognize the prophet until we've listened to the prophetic message with the ear of our heart. This kind of listening is from the core of our being, the affective realm. This is not an intellectual listening. The prophetic moment challenges us to cultivate a deeply listening heart, moving us into deeper reflection and discernment as we wrestle with our response to the prophetic moment. We are stretched to grow in loving awareness and attentiveness, especially to that which was not previously seen. A hospitable heart enables us to hear the voice of the prophet, especially when the message is not easy to hear. The gift of hospitality is that it prepares our hearts, moving us into sufficient self-awareness for reflective receptivity of the prophetic.

Writer Susan Smith reminds us that to be hospitable

> is to empathize with the vulnerability of others and to empower them by creating mutuality in relationship. . . . To be hospitable is to change power over to power with, thereby creating community. . . . Vulnerability is replaced by the solidarity of belonging.[3]

Benedict was concerned about the stranger in need of hospitality. Having no power or prestige, their request for hospitality places them in a vulnerable position. This defenseless stranger may bring the gift of a prophetic moment that calls us deeper into our monastic commitment and our relationship to God, others, and the created world.

The Prophetic

Have you ever heard a word spoken or witnessed an action taken, and experienced the truth and life found in that word deep within your being? I recall one incidence in particular that was piercingly painful but then became intensely freeing for me—a freedom I came to experience at many different levels. In a conversation with a woman theologian from Mexico, I was challenged in my Anglo tendency to subsume all people's life experiences into my own.[4] To be a white North American is not the same as being an Indian living in Peru, which is not the same as being a black favela dweller in Brazil, which is not the same as being an African urban dweller. She has taught me to own and cherish my own story, and to listen carefully to the story of others. She also inadvertently revealed my tendency to want to clean up life's messes and make everything be "okay." I didn't initially want to hear this. My perspective on life was deepened and enriched once I wrestled though this prophetic moment.

Prophets are called at God's initiative, not their own. A prophet does not simply decide one day to become prophet, like beginning a new career. Rather, the prophet is graced to speak the heart and passion of God to a particular people. Prophets are called from the community they are rooted in, for a specific time and message. This call most often comes out of the ordinary and mundane moments of their lives.

In proclaiming the Word of God, the prophet speaks the living Word of God as well as written Sacred Text. The prophet has an ability to see the ordinary in an extraordinary way and to speak to us in a way that stirs our hearts toward change and transformation. It is in our own deep listening and the fruit of lectio that we recognize the voice of the prophet.

Suzanne Mayer tells us that "prophets look with Divine Vision, a peering, searing insight that can penetrate the barrenness and recognize in it potential for life."[5] Their openness allows them to see potentialities and possibilities we miss, unpacking this for us. The prophetic witness to truth is efficacious, taking on a life of its own, stirring us to life and to growth.

The prophet is rooted deeply in a committed prayer relationship and is therefore able to speak what is on God's heart. Mayer tells us that "because of their intimate experience of being God's friend, trustmate, confidant, they could call the people they were sent to serve to a like intimacy, to a community of presence, to a radical change of heart."[6] Prophets show us the way through an efficacious vulnerability cultivated from a raw, honest, and fiery relationship with their Beloved to a wiser understanding of God's call in our life.

Rather than encountering one person whom we might call a prophet, we are more apt to experience the *prophetic moment*: those transforming moments that evoke from us a response toward critical and reflective thinking, a change in the way we make choices. Prophetic moments tend to be social: calling us to establish justice and to build and broaden community toward a more humane ordering of relationships.

Often, the person graced to be the vehicle of a prophetic moment is not aware that she has been particularly called: They are simply speaking deep truth passionately from their hearts. Their strength is in their vulnerability to share their struggles, pain, and hard-won wisdom. I have experienced this in particular with one of my friends: Her willingness to share her intense personal struggles with our culture's bigotry has caused me to reexamine my own assumptions about societal values. I do not see things the same way anymore. I hear differently: The discord of prejudice, especially a subtle and seductive prejudice, has become more evident.

Discernment

In RB 53 we see how movement characterizes Benedict's approach to such issues as the relationship between community and guest, between welcome and caution, reception and separation.[7] Community life is not static, it is a dance. Benedict's desire for welcoming and honoring the Christ within each guest is balanced with a concern for protecting the monastic way of life. Some guests are disruptive through inappropriate behaviors, inordinate demands, violation of boundaries, and vast emotional needs.

My own community extends hospitality within the context of our daily life. Although hospitality is central to our life and ministry, we have a group of Sisters and employees who do the work of hospitality in particular ways. They meet as a committee on a regular basis to coordinate our ministry of hospitality. The community created a safe, inviting, and comfortable space while maintaining the private space of our monastic community. Our guidelines for interacting with retreatants and guests are designed to protect the contemplative space for both so that we do not distract each other.[8]

A community living deeply the charism of hospitality can provide the context and support for discerning the prophetic message and ministry. Personal discernment is a process of seeking wisdom and listening in love in order to clarify God's call in my life. The discernment process uncovers areas of particular freedom and bondage where I have the opportunity to share struggles, to be attentive to movements of the Spirit, and to make choices. In the discernment process, my own heart may be changed, my eyes may see anew, and my ears may be opened and newly attuned to the enlightenment and movement of the Spirit. Communal discernment engages the prophet and the message in a respectful dialogue.

> *Lectio* can give each of us the time and space to put words to our experience, to grasp it better and to become women of wisdom for our community and our Church. A profound personal level of *lectio* in a community is bound to be communicated, leading to a deeper sharing and a keener discernment of what God is asking us now. To the degree that every member of the community is able to speak her wisdom, then to let it go, and to hear and assimilate the wisdom of others, will the group come closer and closer to the will of God on any given issue at any given time in its history.[9]

The community receives the prophetic word and is open to the prophetic moment by supporting and engaging the dance of ongoing discernment. The sincere work of discernment leaves us all changed.

Challenges

Both the *prophet within community* and the *prophet as guest* have their own unique challenges. Each community must discern how it is to create a supportive environment for the prophet within. We need to support and nurture the prophetic gift. Benedict sought to minimize disruptions to community life while maintaining openness to the visit of the prophetic.

Hospitality cultivates the listening heart of the prophet so that the truth can be spoken with gentleness and without crushing the delicate reed. Hospitality gives the prophet space to hear the Spirit and to hear the self, allowing these two voices to dialogue and moving the prophet toward the work of discernment. A safe space is needed for effective discernment. Hospitality provides an accepting, non-judgmental voice to enter into conversation about the calling and the message. Within this space of hospitality, the prophet will encounter someone who will challenge them in an open and receptive way.

The hospitality extended by the monastic community allows the prophet to be nurtured, challenged, supported, and embraced in the midst of the prophetic journey. Our communities can empower the prophet by engaging in conversation. Asking probing, evocative, and clarifying questions helps the prophet better understand the call and message. We also provide the reflective space for the unfolding of unexpected insights from God.

Our communities can provide the physical, psychological, and spiritual space, solitude, and stillness to hear the voice of God. The gifts of hospitality and discernment support the prophet to be wisely sensitive in "choosing one's fights." Speaking the Word of

God has a cost: Wise discernment helps us to see this and to make appropriate choices. The prophet must learn to live with the question and keep the discernment active and ongoing.

Our Reception of the Prophetic

The prophetic word moves us from a static place of orientation toward disorientation and back to reorientation. This prophetic movement confronts our blind spots, prejudices, and presuppositions. It helps us to see and understand systemic injustice, to discern paths toward transformation, and to guide us in a particular action or series of actions toward a change in a way of life. The prophet calls us to stop and look at our lives, our alleged values and choices, and to see something we do not necessarily want to see. The prophet calls us from apathy, stereotyping, exclusivity, and superficiality toward a deeper experience of life. The prophet shows us the available path toward authentic interior freedom and joy. Edwina Gateley reminds us, "The world was not meant to be like this! When we accept the system with our 'this is the way it is,' we become part of it. We are part of the oppression, the injustice, and the diminishment. Blessed are they who never get used to it!"[10]

Integrity calls for the prophet to speak the truth from the heart, in remaining true to self and God. Gateley speaks of the *God of my bellybutton*: We know deep in our guts what we must do, for it is there that God has spoken to us. She speaks of God as the *Divine Thermometer*, not as the *Divine Accountant*: God's "judgment" will focus on our passion for justice and mercy, not how many "little sins" we committed. Hildegard of Bingen, a Benedictine nun of deep passion for the Divine, defined sin as the condition of *drying up!* The prophetic moment can model for us the truth and the power of speaking from our inner being.

The prophet can also gift us by showing us that it is in our woundedness and sin that we draw close to God. The prophet gifts us with opportunities to grow toward a greater interior freedom, to risk following our deepest dreams and passions, to live united to the Absolute in union with our truest selves and in harmony with nature. The prophet calls us from an attitude of scarcity to one of abundance, and to live in relationships that are collaborative and mutually empowering rather than power-over relationships.

The prophet can initially irritate us by calling forth something we do not want to give and challenging us to deep interior work in response. We may not want our security blankets taken from us. Our work of hospitality calls us to engage the prophetic in conversation. Often the prophet does not have the answers, but rather initiates the conversation that moves us toward an answer. We are placed in creative chaos as we struggle with the question.

Extending hospitality to the prophetic can result in our marginalization, as individuals or as community. Offering hospitality to certain people can be counter-cultural and unpopular. We can end up being at odds with religious institutions, popular movements, and the prevailing climate of political correctness.

How does the prophet extend hospitality when there is conflict? The prophet must be vulnerable and listen when engaged in a conversation with the other. This is done with an attitude that honors the person and calls forth the good from the one who may be challenging the message or the messenger. The prophet has an opportunity for growth in extending hospitality in a personally difficult situation.

Journeying With the Prophetic

In companioning the prophet, a spiritual director listens intently for where the Spirit is stirring and calling. She tries to ask evocative questions that stir inner reflection and self-awareness, especially around intuitive feelings and memories. These questions are meant to engage both the head and the heart. Spiritual directors try to provide a supportive and safe environment so that this evocative and discerning process can happen.

In journeying with the prophetic, spiritual directors are called to be especially attentive to issues of self-care and balance, both for the director and the prophet. This self-care and balance are essential if the spiritual director is to be effectively present to the prophet, to hear the message and respond. Both must remain true to self and grounded in community and in God, and embrace inner simplicity and silence. In order to remain rooted and effective, both must remain nourished by the Word, especially through lectio. Lectio prepares the ground of our hearts to be open to the prompting of the Spirit—and especially open to the unexpected.

Spiritual directors are privileged to assist the prophetic seeker in testing the waters of this prophetic call. Where does it come from? Where is the person's identity in the midst of this call? Where is the life, the gratitude and sense of movement? The spiritual director is called to be truly present to the prophet in that moment: listening deeply for shifts, dissonance, and moments that contain energy. These are opportunities to move the discernment into new terrain.

Conclusion

Hospitality, like lectio, prepares our hearts to receive the living Word through the prophetic moment as well as through the work of the prophet. Hospitality in itself has its own charism of the prophetic that may or may not be well received. Hospitality can be the vehicle to keep alive the conversation with the prophetic. Hospitality may also be the fertile ground of nurturing, refining, and focusing the prophetic gift. The prophetic keeps us reflecting upon and deepening our ministry of hospitality. May we keep the conversation going!

Chapter Ten

Justice

The year 1980 was pivotal for many Catholics in North America. In March the beloved and prophetic Monseñor Oscar Romero was coldly assassinated by the U.S. supported Salvadoran military.[1] Could any government, including our own, be a party to the murder of a simple beloved priest and the most senior member of the Salvadoran Roman Catholic Church?

Then December of 1980 arrived. Four American Women—Jean Donovan, Maryknoll Sisters Ita Ford and Maura Clarke, and Ursuline Sister Dorothy Kazel—were kidnapped and executed by the Salvadoran National Guard. The consciousness of Americans, and especially North American Women Religious, was shaken awake. Violently.

Until this time, Americans tended to live with a belief that we were untouchable; no foreign government would kill an American, especially a beloved Catholic Sister. The Holy Spirit woke us from our slumber of indifference. Innocents were being slaughtered over greed for land and political and economic power. Women Religious were executed for sitting with the poor and incarnating the gospel of Jesus. The cost of discipleship, the cost of faithfulness to the missionary call, the cost of standing with the marginalized and silenced was everything.

It was time for us to hear the gospel message; we must now be the listeners and students of those entrusted with the Good News. We must sit quietly and listen to the poor, the diminished, and the outcast. Today's leper must become our teacher and show us the way. With warm and gracious hearts that have overcome the power of despair and hopelessness, with the determination, perseverance, and vision to build a more just and equitable world, the anawim are willing teachers and guides. Will we listen *with the ear of our hearts*? Will we step away from our idols and sit at the feet of those teachers the Holy Spirit has anointed?

Monseñor Oscar Romero was born into a poor and simple family. He was gifted with a passion for books and a love for his people, the poor of El Salvador. His early years serving the Church allowed him to continue his reading and studying. Yet he always had time to visit with the young and old, the sick and the poor. They were his people and he was comfortable in their presence.

Monseñor Romero was a thinking person. As his responsibilities increased, he was confronted with modern contradictions: He initially tended to be conservative, yet the Second Vatican Council and later the work of the bishops gathering at Medellín were challenging the structural causes of poverty.[2] The Church was clearly placing itself on the side of the poor, striving to cultivate a special tenderness. Romero confronted his own interior resistance and made a choice to begin listening to the poor and those, such as Jesuit Father Rutilio Grande, who journeyed closely with them.[3] His own conversion process had begun.

Until he became Archbishop, Romero did not question the structural causes behind the suffering of the poor. He tended to take a passive stance toward poverty rather than looking hard at the causes and solutions of suffering.

Because of his intellectual pursuits, he was perceived as nonthreatening to the ruling elite: the families who controlled the economy and government, the military, and the Church hierarchy of El Salvador. This kind and friendly country bishop was

perceived as an acceptable compromise candidate to become archbishop of San Salvador, the senior prelate of the country.

Then the Holy Spirit forever touched his life. His new position
and the people around him began to challenge his lack of awareness. Romero stepped away from his books and went out to meet
his people. He saw and observed and reflected and prayed. His
keen intellect gave him the power to ask difficult and complex
questions. He acted on his nagging questions and observations.
Each step led to another step—observing, listening, and prayerful
struggle—and soon he was causing trouble for many in power. He
gave much-needed hope to many as he began to embody the true
meaning of being the People of God. Romero spoke from his head
and heart. Until the day when, during the Eucharistic prayer, he
became the ultimate Eucharist. The military shot him as he stood
silent at the altar.[4] Yet Romero does not remain silent.

Ita, Maura, Jean, and Dorothy came to El Salvador, each from
very different lives, to journey with the poor and to discover
together the gospel for their lives. Each was a simple and loving
woman. Each daily became increasingly aware that the innocents
were being hunted down and killed. Those who were murdered
were called *The Disappeared*.

Ita Ford became increasingly vocal in her resistance to the night-
ly forays of the death squads. She frequently confronted the cold-
blooded murderers of their own people. Sister Ita became an
irritant the military decided needed to be removed. She spoke the
truth and it cost her life. Yet each of these women has become the
voice for the more than eighty thousand unnamed Salvadoran victims; they are *resurrection witnesses* to the Salvadoran people that
God has not abandoned them. Their families, religious communities, and friends have not remained silent. Knowing well the
potential cost, the People of God remained steadfast in their journey with the Salvadoran poor and did not leave. Four voices have
been replaced by thousands of voices.

Romero, Ita, Maura, Jean, and Dorothy continue to teach us.
There is no greater joy than following the voice of Jesus; it may
only cost us our lives. Jesus is living for us today in the presence
of the poorest poor and speaks to us through the insignificant and

voiceless. They can show us how the People of God live, the choices that reveal our heart for God and lead us to the fullest of life.

What Is Justice?

Justice encompasses the acts, structures and systems that affirm, support, and defend human dignity and worth. Justice affirms, rather than diminishes, the worth and dignity of all. Justice encourages the pursuit of one's fullest potential as well as the potential of those around us. A justice-oriented life pushes forth to pursue this potential. Justice demands a stance of intense interior listening and awareness of the vulnerable who are in need of protection. Justice is honor and wisdom.

Justice is action. It permeates our being and reveals our truest self. A justice-oriented life is filled with passion, exuberance, and joy. A justice-oriented life helps us discover our truest self.

Justice is the call of all the baptized. It is a gospel mandate for each of us to extend our hearts, minds, and actions toward doing justice. Jesus consistently embodied compassion. A justice-oriented lifestyle is the mark of the follower of Jesus.

As Pastor Jennifer Johnston points out:

> Doing justice, as Walter Brueggemann defines it: . . . "is to sort out what belongs to whom and to return it to them." His definition assumes a right distribution of goods and access to the sources of life. When some have unjustly held certain goods and privileges for a long time, it can seem as though they have always belonged to them. Rarely do we have the opportunity and grace to see the direct costs of our lifestyle on those in other parts of our country or world. . . . How often are we aware to whom this land belongs or who paid the cost of building our economic structures? Seldom do we see in our daily lives to whom what we have in fact belongs. It does

not mean we can remain in postures of privilege. Doing justice is difficult, especially for those of us who have something to lose or have a debt to repay for benefiting from inequality.[5]

Justice work is particularly effective when done in collaboration with one's community, whether this is a monastic community, family, faith community, or a community formed from a particular commitment, such as prison ministry. Healthy human community has a significant potential for fostering conversation around ethics and resulting life choices. We must each discern how we are called to live justly and do justice.

We grow in our understanding and personal call toward justice when we wrestle with our perceptions and presumptions. Every culture has its genius and resistance to incarnating justice in the world. The West has a longstanding tradition around charitable institutions as well as corporate responsibility toward one another, even though lived out imperfectly. Yet we are blinded by concepts of justice, so that see prison as punishment rather than as a means of reform. We execute human life under the excuse of *an eye for an eye*. We can be shortsighted and judgmental when it comes to handling the sinful and severely wounded. We seek immediate answers to challenges that do not have easy solutions. Archbishop Desmond Tutu of South Africa tells us,

> There are different kinds of justice. Retributive justice is largely Western. The African understanding is far more restorative—not so much to punish as to redress or restore a balance that has been knocked askew. The justice we hope for is restorative of the dignity of the people. This is an expression of the African notion of *ubuntu*—interconnectedness, the idea that no one can be healthy when the community is sick. It's a deeply Christian concept. You are not saved as an individual, but through incorporation into a body.[6]

Western concepts of justice need to grow into new understandings and commitments, into resurrection.

Justice needs to be incorporated into the fabric of our daily life. Pastoral theologian Marie Fortune, speaking in reference to her work on behalf of women suffering under domestic and sexual violence, defines justice as:

- *Truth-telling:* in order to break the silence and to speak God's life-giving WORD.
- *Acknowledgment:* listening to the story of the victimized, and affirming the truth of their experience.
- *Compassion:* standing with the victimized; extending a listening ear and a warm heart.
- *Protection of the Vulnerable:* whenever possible, the frail and vulnerable are protected from the perpetrators of injustice.
- *Accountability of the Offender:* Calling the offender(s) to account in any way possible. The community communicates that this harmful behavior must stop.
- *Restitution to the Survivor/Victims:* Compensation for the material cost of the harm done (such as counseling).
- *Vindication for the Survivor:* this is to be literally "set free." Justice enables a survivor to be freed from the burden of memory, self-blame (as most victims do), and pain in order to get on with life.[7]

Justice in the Rule of Benedict

Benedict's Rule is permeated with the early Christian view of justice that is rooted in the Jewish understanding of justice. God is the source and originator of justice. God sets the standard for justice that we need to aspire to. Our hearts and minds are to be imbued with hunger for justice. The Divine dwells in justice. So Benedict merely reminds his followers that justice is core to the monastic way of life.

✠

> We dwell closely to the Holy One when we walk
> blamelessly and act justly, speaking the truth can-
> didly and not having committed fraud with our
> tongue, doing no ill nor listening to slander against
> our neighbors (Prologue 25–26).

Benedict reminds us that any person who yearns to draw close to God will act with justice. This includes both deeds of justice as well as a healthy relationship with others. Doing justice, especially when there is a price to be paid, opens the heart to hear the voice of the Holy One. The cost of justice may mean attending to our attachments, prejudices, self-will, or self-centeredness. For North Americans this cost is often economic, as we redistribute wealth to those in need. Just choices and actions literally move us toward the Holy One.

✠

> Let the orders and teachings of our monastic leader
> be kneaded into our minds as disciples like the leav-
> en of divine justice (RB 2:5).

Leaven transforms the raw ingredients into bread. Good leaven will produce delightful bread with good texture; bad leaven will produce heavy, raunchy bread or even kill the batter completely. But it will transform.

The monastic way involves a transformation of heart. The oblate or monastic makes a promise that includes fidelity to the monastic way of life. This involves a daily journey to root out all attachments, resentment, bitterness, unhealthy attitudes—literally everything—that keeps one from an intimate and intense relationship with the Holy One. Monastics have walked with their prioress or abbot in a pastoral relationship. The Holy Spirit sometimes moves within that relationship in surprising and strange ways.

✠

*Their shepherd will be absolved in God's judgment,
and may say to the Holy One with the Prophet: I
have not hidden your justice in my heart. I have proclaimed your truth and your salvation, but they have
mockingly rejected me* (RB 2:9).

The Rule presumes that justice is not merely pretty ideas or
pleasant thoughts. Justice is something we do. The monastic way
understands that some of our conversion of heart takes place
when we make personally difficult choices in the service of justice.
Actions are first and the feelings will follow. Justice is a vehicle of
transformation on every level. Our lives must be a proclamation of
just relationships.

✠

Bear persecution on behalf of justice (RB 4:33).

Early Christians understood that justice is countercultural and
can earn us enemies. Doing justice can leave us on the outskirts of
society, and hence we can lose benefits of our society. Benedict is
lifting a passage from the Sermon on the Mount that Benedictine
scholar Terrence Kardong calls a "nonviolent resistance."[8]
Persecution can result from the pursuit of justice, yet we are called
to remain faithful despite difficulties. Benedict expects his followers to cultivate a just heart, although we may pay a price.
Ultimately we reap more—a deep relationship with God and
healthy relationships with other people enlivened—than is
surrendered.

✠

*If some work of the artisans is to be sold, those who
are to transact the sale should be careful not to presume to engage in any deception. . . . The evil of
avarice ought not to creep into these prices. Rather,
they should sell things a little more cheaply than*

secular can. And so God will be glorified in all things (RB 57:4, 7–9).

In Benedict's day, monastics benefited their regions by making and offering products for lower prices, allowing the poorer access to some of life's gifts. The livelihood of most people was based on agriculture and created goods accessible only by the very few. Our economics are drastically different today. Our modern ears could come to understand Benedict as telling his followers to become ruthless, cutthroat marketers.

We live in a world fully saturated with materialism. We are hit from every angle with sophisticated media assaults, aiming to convince us that their products are essential. We have seen the rise of predatory businesses whose marketing techniques target the young and drive out small businesses. These are the familiar huge stores that sell for less by purchasing products made by children and virtual slave labor.

There are creative ways that one can apply Benedict's principles to our current economic climate. Some options are buying products manufactured by labor-friendly businesses, conducting our business locally, and seriously questioning the amount of our purchasing. We can avoid businesses associated with inhumane manufacturing practices, such as paying grossly low wages, maintaining unsafe working conditions, and devastating the environment.

Justice calls us toward paying just wages and providing just and healthy working conditions and adequate support for families. Churches and Religious Communities can seek funding for what is truly needed, not merely wanted. Our call is to empower the voiceless and marginalized—not contribute further to their marginalization by ruthless business practices.

That the Whole Fulfillment of Justice Is Not Laid Down in This Rule

✠

We have sketched out this Rule, so that carrying it out in monasteries we may at least show that we have moral decency and the rudiments of a monastic life. But for someone who is in a hurry to reach the fullness of monastic life, there are the teachings of the Holy Fathers and Mothers. Anyone who carries them out will arrive at the pinnacle of perfection. For what page or even what word of the divinely inspired Hebrew and Christian Testaments is not a completely reliable guidepost for human life? Or what book of the holy Catholic writers does not teach us how to reach our Creator by the direct route? And then there are the *Conferences* and their *Institutes* and *Lives*, along with the Rule of our Holy Father Basil. What are they for monastics who live upright and obedient lives but tools of virtue (RB 73)?

Kardong points out that this section of the Rule is grounded in the Gospel of Matthew, where justice is based on covenant relationship, not "rights."[9] *Sedekah*, the Hebrew root word for justice, refers to the covenant relation between Yahweh and the chosen people, not extensive pious observances. Benedict expects his followers to live a life that is essentially grounded in an intimate love for God; justice flows from this covenant relationship.

Justice is the natural result of a heart steeped in God. Benedict exhorts his followers, impelled by a personal experience of God's love for us, to immerse ourselves in sacred scripture and the teachings of monastic tradition until they permeate every aspect of our being. Justice comes more naturally from a heart steeped in God's truth. Attitudes, motives, and thoughts become justice-oriented.

Who Are the People of God?

One of the great modern theologians, Jesuit Father Ignacio Ellacuría defined the People of God as those who seek to fulfill the work initiated by Jesus Christ.[10] The People of God define the identity and authenticity of the Church by their acts of justice and liberation. Our behavior can express the passion and mission of the Church to love as Christ loved. Theologian María Pilar Aquino explained Ellacuría's thinking:

> In a world imprisoned by injustice, the true People of God embody the self of the true Church precisely in its struggles against all forms of injustice so that the world becomes the historical manifestation of a new earth and a new humanity, liberated from individual egotism and from the sin of injustice.[11]

Ellacuría's People of God are those who are empowered by the Holy Spirit to establish justice where injustice rules. He defined the People of God as:
- Those who are innocent but suffer the costs of a society's sin (the poorest of the poor / the anawim).
- Those who actively seek the Reign of God on earth.
- All those who struggle for liberation and the transformation of this hurting world into a new creation in which the whole of humanity lives with dignity.
- Those whose work opens the way to lasting peace and true reconciliation.
- Those who live the fundamental virtues of the Christian faith: compassion and mercy for those who suffer, faith in the essential value and prophetic power of the impoverished, and hope that sees beyond the injustice of the present and fights for something better in this world; hope that trusts in the resurrection.
- Those who live in a process of conversion to God, who seek revelation among those who are working to save the world from injustice.[12]

For Ellacuría, the People of God reveal the truth and depth of the gospel in their daily dedication to journey with the poorest of God's children. God's people lovingly challenge those who hold wealth and power to use their resources in ways that serve the dignity of all people and protect the natural world. We are called to challenge the growing tendency toward a distorted sense of personal entitlement and greed with a more humane and democratic vision of community. Many who cooperate and perpetrate injustice and systemic injustice secretly yearn to discover and live by their God-created values. They may yearn to become more whole.

The People of God are a resurrection people. Challenges, defeats, thwarted plans, hopes, and aspirations do not end in death, even physical death. Persecution affirms the power of living truth. Persecution comes from speaking and living the truth in the face of systemic injustice. Resurrection—the total transformation of every aspect of life into what God originally intended for all of us—is the ultimate destiny of the People of God. Aware of the threats against his life, Archbishop Oscar Romero once declared:

> I must tell you that as a Christian I do not believe in death without resurrection. If they kill me, I will rise again in the Salvadoran people. . . . May my death, if it is accepted by God, be for the liberation of my people and as a witness of hope in the future. . . . Better, of course, that they realize that they will be wasting their time. A bishop will die, but God's Church, which is the people, will never perish.[13]

The People of God recognize that all people are more important and valuable than any bureaucratic institution: government, business, or the Church. Many who faithfully serve in the institutional Church today anguish over the tensions between the institution and tradition, and the yearnings of God's People for the fullness of life.

The People of God are not persecuted or martyred for defending dogma or institutional privileges, but for incarnating Christian virtues, particularly for standing with the poor and persecuted.[14]

The Church is fulfilling its purpose when it uses social pressure as a unified faith community to heal the world's suffering. The result of this daily commitment to justice and defense of human dignity has been confrontation with those who hold power, whether political or economic. At times one must confront systems of injustice directly, at other times the confrontation may be indirect.

> The true People of God in a world dominated by sin cannot but be persecuted. . . . First of all there is the persecution of the people, a persecution that at its root is that of structural oppression and then becomes repression when the people have become conscious and have organized struggles for liberation. Then comes the persecution of the People of God, which seeks to bring salvation history into the history of the People of God and integrate the history of the people into salvation history.[15]

The People of God call each member of society to their better selves, their greatest dignity. We must teach those who perpetuate unjust structures that diminish the humanity of the vulnerable that when any one of us diminishes the other, we diminish ourselves.

The powerful tend to be blind to the advantages of disengaging from unjust social structures. They benefit financially from increased profit margins by paying unjust wages, tolerating unhealthy and unsafe working conditions, and in plundering the environment with an unlimited demand for natural resources. Violence results: toward human life, the environment, and in the social and political realm.

Of the vicious cycle of violence, Dr. Martin Luther King, Jr., taught us:

> The ultimate weakness of violence is that it is a descending spiral, begetting the very thing it seeks to destroy. Instead of diminishing evil, it multiplies it. Through violence you murder the hater, but you do not murder hate. In fact, violence merely increases

hate. . . . Returning violence for violence multiplies violence, adding deeper darkness to a night already devoid of stars. Darkness cannot drive out darkness; only light can do that. Hate cannot drive out hate; only love can do that.

Love is the only force capable of transforming an enemy into a friend. . . . By its very nature, hate destroys and tears down; by its very nature, love creates and builds up. Love transforms with redemptive power.[16]

There are opportunities to pursue life-giving paradigms. New, hope-filled ways can be found to serve the human family. We can open our hearts to embrace the diversity of culture and we learn from those who are different from us. As our God is one of abundance, we are content in simplicity and reject the lie of the Evil One revealed in an attitude of scarcity.

Ellacuría believed that people can attain salvation without an explicit confession of faith but we cannot be saved without doing justice.

The fullness of Christian faith is not only surrender to God, acceptance of God's revealing communication and the embracing of a supernatural dynamism, but it is also a new way of life that necessarily includes the doing of justice; and in turn, the doing of justice is a way of knowing God . . . it is more evident that there is no faith without justice than justice without faith.[17]

Monastic Justice

The call to justice is a Biblical mandate. Our hearts and minds will be shaped by our commitment to justice. Justice needs to be as natural to our life as breathing. Each of us must discern our particular call to works of justice.

The monastic shares this human call to justice. There is a long tradition of justice in the monastic call. Monasteries sheltered the pilgrim, fed the hungry, cared for the sick, and educated local children. There may be particularly monastic ways of doing justice. The context of the monastic pursuit of justice is particularized in the balance between ancient monastic tradition and contemporary realities. Every individual and every monastic community discerns their particular call to justice with each generation.

Monastics hunger for silence and solitude. In the place of intense silence we encounter our heart's deepest longing for the Holy One. In the silence we experience compassion and pain: God's own yearning for justice. We dare to feel with God, which requires the courageous receptivity of Mary's Magnificat. Listening in the depths of personal and communal silence demands of us the willingness to hear what we do not want to hear: the painful, the fearful, and the challenging.

Monastics help others to hear the voice of God. In our ministries of spiritual direction (or spiritual companioning); in our education and pastoral ministry; and in our writing, preaching, and artwork; we can present opportunities for wise listening. It is equally important that monastics place themselves in a position to listen to the cries of despair and hopelessness. We must listen and ask the piercing question, for ourselves and others.

Monastics ask evocative, perceptive, challenging, and discerning questions. We have many opportunities to welcome conversations around justice.[18] A few powerful voices have been dominating this conversation for too long: setting the agenda, defining and controlling truth, and too often confusing the cultural with the Will of God. Benedictines model differently. We can encourage the imaginative and creative ways of doing theology, of being Church, and of reaching out to a world in pain. We can encourage conversations that explore new possibilities and help us all see with fresh eyes.

Monasteries have an opportunity to embody collaboration, interdependence in community. Mutual obedience and collaborative leadership are models of new ways of relating to power. Our monasteries can honor diversity, build communication, and effectively handle conflict.

Benedictines are challenged to move out of our comfort zones and be touched by the pain of the marginalized. We must allow ourselves to feel anger and helplessness, for it is there that we are truly listening into conversion. María Pilar Aquino tells us,

> Theology claiming to be above history, or theology that is not conscious of its premises, ends up identifying with the dominant power in the church and society. This is to its own detriment and humanity's, because such a theology ignores the questions and deepest desires of the majority of human beings: the poor and oppressed of the earth. It becomes deaf to the urgent cries by victims of injustice claiming their right to life.[19]

Monastics do not have the luxury of identifying with the dominant power. Benedict began a lay and nonclerical movement that stripped those who joined him of the vestiges of their social standing. He continues to teach us how to pursue God, not political power, especially within the Church.

Theological reflection must be grounded in a deepening awareness of our own poverty and oppression. Our awareness must be grounded in vulnerability and a willingness to journey with the oppressed, letting their cries of despair and anguish pierce our hearts. We are called to be, in the words of Aquino, the *paschal continuity*.

A Spirituality of Justice

Doing justice as a way of life is

> the source and expression of a profound Christian spirituality that is grounded on the truth of the

Gospel. The faith lived by the People of God in the context of *the kingdom of hell* can only operate as a *principle of liberation*.[20]

Resurrection is experienced as injustice is eliminated.

If you are neutral in a situation of injustice, you have chosen the side of the oppressor. If an elephant has his foot on the tail of the mouse, and you say you are neutral, the mouse will not appreciate your neutrality (Desmond Tutu).

Passivity as a way of avoiding conflict or commitment is not an option. Pondering and discerning until we understand our call is our first response to justice. Silence is the place where we encounter the Divine, but it is not meant to be a way of avoiding commitment to justice. Silence needs to be well focused, not self-serving or self-preserving! Then it carries weight and voice and history, a silence grounded in wisdom.

If we are not aware of our own cultural biases and assumptions, we can fail to hear others because of the loud voices within. We need to enter into dialogue with confidence and trust. The conversation must be inclusive and yet we must allow differences to remain differences; we must not try to fix things up. Differences need not be perceived as threats. It is possible to listen and seek to understand their values, hopes, and fears; to stand in their shoes.

At times it is easy to shut out others who are different because what they say exposes something that we do not want to see. The challenge is to maintain a stance of openness, vulnerability, and a willingness to stay with the conversation for as long as needed. Western culture tends to value efficiency. Staying with the conversation, for however long it takes, can be very difficult. Monastic communities can help to sustain the conversation, moving it toward depth and breadth.

Justice Spirituality

Justice Spirituality is expressed in our awareness of our connection and interdependence with all others and creation. A sense of empowerment and affirmation of our dignity results. Justice Spirituality supports peace in the face of violence. Living justice fosters a deep and abiding compassion and enables us to see with new eyes. Any degree of violence becomes intolerable. We begin to counteract violence by standing for peace and defending others.

Justice Spirituality expresses love, joy, hope, and mercy; each a transformative force. The pursuit of justice can cause despair or envy or a desire for vengeance. We must be careful that we do not perpetuate oppression by dominating, controlling, speaking for others, or manipulating. Faith sustains the pursuit of justice. Discerning the movement of the Holy Spirit sustains our joy and the abundance of God's gifts.

The dominant culture equated its own culture with Christianity, and abusive practices often resulted. Inculturation does not mean that we lose our distinctive cultural ways of expressing our Christian faith. "We must maintain the radical distinction between the Gospel message and any culture . . . faith in Christ is not the product of any culture; its origin lies in a divine revelation."[21] Besides faith, family, and friends, the greatest gift we inherit at birth is the culture we are born into. Our faith, however, finds meaningful expression in every culture. Our God sings many songs.

Living lectio helps us ponder the commitment to justice in our own lives. Do I dwell in the midst of a healthy community? How am I challenged to support a justice-oriented life? How do I use resources to empower the anawim? How do I risk challenging others in my community toward self-care and justice work?

In what concrete ways am I allowing myself to be taught by the anawim? What defense mechanisms do I use to protect my heart from being pierced by their message? Do I have the courage to risk dropping these defense mechanisms?

Do I own my possessions—or do they own me? Am I a clutter addict? Am I free to give away what I am currently using? What methods do I use to scrutinize what I am holding onto and what I give away? Am I satisfied or dissatisfied? What corner of my world is the Holy Spirit calling me to renew with justice?

Notes

CHAPTER ONE: BENEDICT AND THE MONASTIC TRADITION

1. The Abbey of Monte Cassino was the last of many monasteries established by Saint Benedict. It is here that he finished writing his Rule and died in 547 C.E.
2. Exodus 17:12.
3. RB 48:1, 4, 5, 10, 13, 23.
4. RB 2:16–22; 21:4; 63.
5. RB 23 and 27.
6. See McNamara, *Sisters in Arms*; Elm, *"Virgins of God"*; Dunn, *Emergence of Monasticism*; Swan, *Forgotten Desert Mothers*; Krawiec, *Shenoute*; and Harrington, *Women in a Celtic Church* as initial sources for studying the beginnings of the monastic movement in Christianity.
7. Kardong, *Benedict's Rule*, 36. My translations are for inclusivity.
8. Ibid., 39.
9. While basic structures of the Liturgy of the Hours remains constant between monasteries, some choose to pray in Latin using Gregorian Chant, others pray in the vernacular with Plain Chant. Some monasteries pray three or four offices, while others pray seven; each community determines the *horarium* or schedule of the monastery. There might be some variance around when and where silence is observed, when Chapters meetings are scheduled and how they are conducted, how special feasts and Jubilees are celebrated, and when work, play, and leisure are scheduled.
10. See I. Howard Marshall, and others, eds., *New Bible Dictionary* (Downers Grove, IL: Intervarsity Press, 1996) for a good introduction to this literary form.
11. Note especially Psalm 34 in the Prologue of RB. See Craghan, *The Psalms*, for an excellent study of the psalms.
12. See also Fry, and others, eds., *RB 1980*, 145, 324–325; see Gregory the Great, *Life of Saint Benedict*.

13. See Deutsch, *Lady Wisdom*, particularly chapter 2.
14. The Latin *schola*, or school, is a place of learning and exploration. For Benedict, the monastic is always in the process of learning and stretching and growing; it is a way of life. See Prologue 45, 49, 50; 1:4–5; 4:75–78.
15. See Kardong, *Benedict's Rule*, 97–98.
16. For those readers who would like to look up references, I include the following sample. For "local conditions": RB 34:4, 5; 40:5, 8; 48:7; 55:1–3, 7; 65:14–15. On "adaptability": Prologue 24; 2:23, 24, 32; 11:11–13; 13:1–2; 17:5–6; 18:22–23; 21:1; 22:3; 24:1; 27:2–3; 31:17; 34:1–5; 39:1–2, 6, 10–11; 41:4–5; 43:10–12; 48:9, 23–25; 53:17–19; 55:20–22; 61:1–4; 64:17–19; 68; 73.
17. See Robinson, *Family Cloister*.
18. RB 8–20. *Opus Dei* means literally the Work of God; today we use the terms Liturgy of the Hours or Divine Office.
19. RB 39, 40, 41, 48 and 55, respectively.
20. McClure and Ramsay, *Telling the Truth*, 39.
21. Doctor Jeanette Rodriguez is a professor at Seattle University. My understandings of "cultural memory" come from our private conversations and her unpublished writings.
22. By "public prayer" I mean the Mass or other Sunday services.
23. Pfatteicher, *Liturgical Spirituality*, 24.
24. Today, these monastic stages of incorporation generally are affiliate, postulant or candidate, novice, initial profession, and perpetual profession.
25. Although no known extant copies exist, women's monastic communities certainly had their own Rules and living traditions. Some women's communities also probably adopted and adapted Rules from neighboring communities of men.

CHAPTER TWO: BENEDICT'S GOOD MONASTIC

1. Based on the prior monastic texts of Jerome, Cassian, and the Master, Benedict placed his understanding of cenobitic monasticism within the monastic tradition of his day. See Kardong, *Benedict's Rule*, 42–45. See also Cassian's Conferences 18:4–8 (see Ramsey, *John Cassian: The Conference*); Jerome's Epistle 22.34 (*Ancient Christian Writers* 33, Letters 1–2) and Eberle, *Rule of the Master*, chapter 1.
2. RB 4:78.
3. RB 72:5.
4. To be fully immersed in prayer, and therefore in the presence of God, was to become as fire. See Swan, *Forgotten Desert Mothers*, especially chapter 2.
5. Solitude requires healthy interior discipline, a strong sense of self-worth, and confidence. In addition, some people experience depression or get in touch with suppressed memories when they begin a practice of meditation and/or periods of intentional solitude. Counseling can be a very helpful tool for learning and integrating these practices of solitude and meditation.
6. The Latin text of RB 1:13 reads *coenobitarum fortissimum*, which would literally read *cenobites, the most vigorous.* Adalbert de Vogüé translates this phrase *cenobites, the very powerful* or *cenobites, the valiant.* See de Vogüé, *Rule of Benedict*, 45, 49; and *Reading Saint Benedict*, 41. Benedict was passionate and fiery in his preferences.
7. While Benedict certainly had a tender heart for those without basic material necessities, "the poor" is inclusive of those ostracized by society, those with no means of defense (in court, in economics, etc.), the vulnerable (such as the disabled, developmentally delayed, the infirm), and the emotionally paralyzed; RB 52.
8. RB 68.
9. Prologue 9–13, 24. We will return to monastic listening in chapter 4 on Obedience.
10. RB 6.
11. RB 43.
12. RB 43:13, 17.

13. Kardong, *Benedict's Rule*, 373.
14. RB 43:13, 17. See Kardong, *Benedict's Rule*, 358–359, 372–373.
15. RB 43:1–3, RB 45, RB 47, RB 52, RB 67.
16. Prologue 4 and RB 20.
17. We will return to this subject in chapter 3.
18. RB 21:1; RB 21:4, RB 64:2; RB 31:1.
19. Prologue 3; RB 3:8, 9.
20. RB 31.
21. RB 1:5.
22. RB 35:1, RB 36.
23. RB 31:9, RB 36, RB 66:1; RB 36, RB 64:12, 13.
24. RB 72:5.
25. RB 64.
26. RB 72.
27. RB 4:50, RB 7:44, RB 46:5ff.
28. RB 45, RB 46.
29. The monastic promise is understood as the total giving of self to God in the monastery. It includes stability (I will seek God in this place and with this group of monastics), fidelity to the monastic way of life (a commitment to learn and grow and mature) and obedience (a commitment to individual and group discernment); Prologue, RB 1:1–5, and RB 58 on entrance and profession.
30. RB 48.
31. RB 33; RB 34, RB 54, RB 55.
32. RB 55:18.
33. RB 72:7, 8.

CHAPTER THREE: UNTIL IT SOAKS INTO MY BONES: BENEDICT ON PRAYER

1. For example, see RB 4:48–49; 7:10–30, 62–64.
2. Prologue 4; RB 19:1; RB 20:2; RB 20:3–5.
3. RB 43:3 reads: *Therefore nothing should be put ahead of the Work of God.*
4. RB 58:7 reads: *You must note whether s/he really seeks God, and whether s/he is serious about the Work of God.*
5. RB 43:1–3 reads: *At the time for the Divine Office, as soon as you hear the signal, drop whatever is in hand and rush there with*

the greatest haste. We should do so with dignity so as not to provide an occasion for silliness. Therefore nothing should be put ahead of the Work of God.

6. RB 9:7 reads: *As soon as the cantor begins to sing "Glory be to the Creator," let all the monastics rise from their seats in honor and reverence for the Holy Trinity.* RB 19:7 reads: *and let us stand to sing in such a way that our mind is in harmony with our voice.*

7. Liturgical seasons include Ordinary Time, Lent, Easter, Pentecost, Advent, and Christmas.

8. Nowell, "Psalms: Living Water," 23.

9. See Brueggemann, *Praying the Psalms* and Swan, *Forgotten Desert Mothers.*

10. Western Civilization is currently understood as western Europe, the United States and Canada, Australia, New Zealand, and English-speaking South Africa.

11. Psalm 58:6; Psalm 59:13.

12. Based on a retreat given at Saint Placid Priory, Lacey, Washington, in June of 2001. McKenna is the author of many books; see the Bibliography for a listing of some of her titles.

13. We too easily forget that the original texts were in Hebrew and Greek. Jesus himself most likely spoke Aramaic; so the translations began with the first written texts.

14. Hume, *Mystery of the Cross,* 3.

15. Isaiah 55:11 (NRSV).

16. Exodus 3:14, from several translations.

17. Currently also known as spiritual mentoring, *anam cara,* or life coaching.

CHAPTER FOUR: IN THE HEART OF COMMUNITY: BENEDICT ON OBEDIENCE

1. For an excellent discussion on this progression from modernity to postmodernity with resulting impact on Religious Life and the life of the Church, see Schneiders, *Finding the Treasure,* especially chapter 3. I rely heavily on her work here.

2. Schneiders, *Finding the Treasure,* 112–113.

3. For an excellent discussion of the "enforced removal" of faith from the public sphere, see Stephen L. Carter, *The Culture of Disbelief: How American Law and Politics Trivialize Religious Devotion* (New York: Basic Books, 1993).

4. Schneiders refers to those who embrace postmodernism as "nihilistic"' or "radically deconstructive postmoderns"; Schneiders refers to those who reject postmodernism as "nostalgic postmoderns."

5. Bongie, *Life of Syncletica*, 61.

6. See Kardong, *Benedict's Rule*, 5; and Böckmann, *Perspektiven der Regula Benedicti*, 20.

7. Ibid., 24.

8. Kardong, *Benedict's Rule*, 7.

9. Ibid., 8–9.

10. Trappist monk Thomas Keating, O.S.C.O., defines a true monastic as one who does not need to be so called.

11. The term "monastic leader" is gender-neutral; Benedict is referring to the prioress or abbot of the monastery. For others, this might be a mentor, pastor, parents; whomever we have a spiritually formative relationship.

12. See Kardong, *Benedict's Rule*, 108.

13. Psychologist D.W.W. Winnicott relates laziness to perfectionism.

14. RB 5:12. See Kardong, *Benedict's Rule*, 115.

15. de Vögué, *Rule of Saint Benedict*, 91.

16. See Böckmann, "Wenn einem Bruder," 5–21; and Kardong, *Benedict's Rule*, 572.

19. Kardong, *Benedict's Rule*, 581; Fry, et al., *RB 1980*, 293.

CHAPTER 5: HUMILITY: CONTEMPORARY CONSIDERATIONS

1. Amma Syncletica was an early desert ascetic. For her Sayings, see Bongie, *Life of Syncletica* and Swan, *Forgotten Desert Mothers*; Evagrius Ponticus was an early mystical theologian; Cassian (approximately 360–435 C.E.) was a monk and prolific writer on the monastic way.

2. The Master, the unknown monastic author of *The Rule of the Master*, massively restructured Cassian's *Institutes* (4.39) in

developing his ladder and instructions on the virtue of humility. Benedict then made changes, mostly toward simplification, in *The Rule of Benedict*.

3. See de Vogüé, *Rule of Benedict*, chapter 7, especially 118.
4. I first encountered the image of a helix in the writings of Robert Kegan, professor at Harvard University, in his groundbreaking work on human development theory. I appreciated his willingness to engage the challenge of women colleagues regarding the lack of serious consideration of women's unique perspectives and issues on personality development. His response was his seminal work, *The Evolving Self*. I especially appreciate the reality that human development is not linear, clean, neat, or tidy.
5. The "new science" is a reference to the recent discoveries and emerging thinking in quantum physics, chaos theory and biology; Wheatley and Kellner-Rogers, *Simpler Way*, 13.
6. Wheatley and Kellner-Rogers, *Simpler Way*, 88.
7. See Swan, *Forgotten Desert Mothers* and Elm, "*Virgins of God.*" Each contains bibliographies for further research. This dualism, based on Greek philosophy and later neo-gnosticism, created a body-mind-spirit split. Benedict was clearly familiar with earlier teachings on humility, especially those of his predecessors: Cassian and the Master. He, too, was writing his Rule for his monastic community of men.
8. Men as well as women are harmed by patriarchy and by the sin of pride. The paradox is that pride for men is the distorted sense of his importance and entitlement that patriarchy granted him. For women, pride is believing and perpetuating the lie that she is irrelevant, unimportant, and worthless. Both patriarchal and matriarchal systems are power-over; the gospel call is to mutuality, interdependence, and collaboration.
9. Glaz and Moessner, *Women in Travail*, 215.
10. Luke 6:29 (NRSV).
11. Saussy, *God Images*, 39.
12. Kegan, *The Evolving Self*, 110.
13. See Gilligan, *In a Different Voice*.

14. There have been numerous models of human personality development, including those by Erik Erikson, J. W. Fowler, and George Valliant.
15. This is currently the final stage of human development (Kegan's stage 5). With current studies of our aging population, this may be revised.
16. Horst, *Recovering the Lost Self*, 14–15.
17. Glaz and Moessner, *Women in Travail*, 113.
18. Saussy, *God Images*, 34.
19. Wheatley and Kellner-Rogers, *Simpler Way*, 3.
20. See Jean Baker Miller, "The Construction of Anger in Women and Men," in Jordan, *Women's Growth*; see also Saussy, *Gift of Anger*.
21. Jean Baker Miller defines "empowering" as increasing the other's resources, capabilities, effectiveness, and ability to act.
22. Jordan, *Women's Growth*, 93.
23. Brock, *Journeys by Heart*, 26.
24. Gilson, *Eros Breaking Free*, 75.
25. Ibid.
26. Brock, *Journeys by Heart*, 34.
27. Gilson, *Eros Breaking Free*, 75.
28. See Peterson, *At Personal Risk*.
29. Children have little voice or choice. Their vulnerability and need for protection are absolute. Rather, I am referring to capable adults.
30. RB 48.
31. RB 34.
32. RB 36.

CHAPTER SIX: BENEDICT'S LADDER OF HUMILITY RE-CONSIDERED

1. Some of the more lengthy steps of humility are abbreviated here. If the reader wants to know the full text, follow along with a copy of Benedict's Rule in hand.
2. See de Vogüé, *Rule of Benedict*, chapter 7; Kardong, "Biblical Roots on Fear"; and Kardong "Clarifications on Humility."
3. de Vogüé, *Rule of Benedict*, 124.
4. Women have been doing theology in the Christian tradition since Mary of Nazareth's encounter with the angel Gabriel when she proclaimed the Magnificat!
5. Horst, *Recovering the Lost Self*, 31–32.
6. Moessner, *Eyes of Women*, 304.
7. Most contemporary cultures do this. When women silence their truest selves, harmful behaviors often result. Hence the rise of eating disorders, domestic violence, sexual assault, teen sexual activity, and the acceptance of degrading pornography.
8. Moessner, *Eyes of Women*, 307.
9. Gilson, *Eros Breaking Free*, 112.
10. See "With a Listening Heart: A Statement on the Role of Discernment in the Lives of American Benedictine Women," in Conference of Prioresses, *Upon This Tradition*.
11. See Heyward, *Touching Our Strength*, especially 104–106.
12. Anyone not Roman was referred to as a "barbarian," usually from one of the Germanic tribes from the north.
13. Medieval mystic Julian of Norwich said: "All shall be well, all shall be well, and in all manner of things, all shall be well." She said this in the midst of the Black Plague that was devastating the population!
14. Horst, *Recovering the Lost Self*, 32–33.
15. In private conversations, some Benedictine men have suggested to me that Benedict was doing a "particularly guy thing" here. They suggest that males need to be shaken awake from their positions of privilege and from the competitiveness in which many men get trapped. If a woman's growth into humility begins with the acceptance of her goodness, then possibly for men, it is to recognize that they

are not the center of the universe and that their relationships with others are not about "winning and defeating."

16. Wheatley and Kellner-Rogers, *Simpler Way*, 61.
17. See Kardong, *Benedict's Rule*, 155–156 for a nice discussion
    of this.
18. See chapter 2.
19. When we internalize the traditions of our family, culture,
    faith, and/or religious community, we value and take own-
    ership for its present and future. Family, culture, and com-
    munity become an extension of who we are. Wandering,
    self-willed monastics had not internalized the values of the
    way of life that their monastic garb proclaimed.
20. See Kardong, *Benedict's Rule*, 156.
21. RB 6, On Silence.
22. See Wink, *Engaging the Powers*, for an excellent, contempo-
    rary exploration of the reality of evil and a more helpful,
    effective understanding of "the Evil One."
23. Gilson, *Eros Breaking Free*, 112.
24. The anawim are the voiceless, the marginalized and power-
    less that are fully dependent on the mercy of others. Today's
    anawim might include people with HIV/AIDS, the unedu-
    cated, single mothers of young children, prisoners and
    especially those on death row, immigrants and children. By
    virtue of baptism, we are called to disengage from all cul-
    tural trappings that keep us separated from the anawim
    and to begin journeying with them.
25. Saussy, *Gift of Anger*, 154.

CHAPTER SEVEN: LENTEN CONSIDERATIONS

1. RB 49.
2. RB 49:7.
3. The Triduum, meaning "space of three days" in reference to
   the days before Easter, is Holy Thursday, Good Friday, and
   Holy Saturday.
4. Kardong, *Benedict's Rule*, 84.
5. Prologue 1.

6. The liturgical seasons provide a nice balance to significant, recurring human experiences. While Lent is about an intense listening, Advent is a time for intense waiting.
7. Prologue 49.
8. RB 72:2–3.

CHAPTER EIGHT: HOLY WEEK PILGRIMAGE

1. *Holy Monotony* is a respectful phrase. The monastic practice of praying the Liturgy of the Hours daily can, at times, have a sense of Holy Monotony. This is because the routine of prayer and praying the psalms in particular become so very familiar to us.
2. There is a kind of spirituality that focuses on pain and suffering as one's sole deserving lot in this life; without intending it, these people deny the reality of resurrection. God intends resolution and reconciliation . . . resurrection.
3. Oscar Romero, *The Violence of Love* (Farmington, PA: Plough, 1988/1998), 131. Translation adapted by the author for inclusivity. The Archbishop of San Salvador, El Salvador, Romero was assassinated on March 24, 1980.

CHAPTER NINE: HOSPITALITY AND THE PROPHETIC

1. See Kardong, *Benedict's Rule*, 435.
2. Kardong, *Benedict's Rule*, 422. See also Kardong, "To Receive All," 195–207.
3. Smith, "Household of God," 41–42.
4. *Anglo* is a term to describe all Americans of Western European descent, although Anglos are from culturally diverse backgrounds themselves.
5. Mayer, *Celebrating the Woman*, 51.
6. Ibid., 52.
7. See Huerre, "Monastic Hospitality."
8. Saint Ignatius of Loyola called distraction *an evil under the guise of a good.*

9. Conference of Prioresses, "With a Listening Heart," in *Upon This Tradition*, 150.
10. Gateley, *Warm, Moist, Salty God*, 29–30.

CHAPTER TEN: JUSTICE

1. The United States government supported the Salvadoran military in its war against the poor to the tune of approximately 1.5 million U.S. dollars daily!
2. A gathering of Central and South American Bishops at Medellín, Columbia, in 1968 produced a significantly important set of documents that proclaimed the Church's preferential option for the poor.
3. Monseñor Romero became a close friend with Rutilio Grande, S.J., assassinated by the Salvadoran military in 1977. Many believe Grande's death marked the beginning of Romero's public defense of the poor.
4. Archbishop Oscar Romero was celebrating Mass at the Hospital Divina Providencia at the request of a reporter hired to assist the military in arranging his assassination. A single bullet to the head killed him. Witnesses claim that after he was shot, Romero bowed to the consecrated host and then dropped quietly to the ground.
5. Jennifer Johnson in Milhaven, *Sermons Seldom Heard*, 57.
6. Rosenberg, "Recovering from Apartheid," 90.
7. See McClure and Ramsay, *Telling the Truth*, 54. Marie Fortune is an ordained minister, author, and the founder of The Center for the Prevention of Sexual and Domestic Violence in Seattle, Washington.
8. Kardong, *Benedict's Rule*, 86.
9. See Kardong, "Justitia," 43–73; see also Kardong, *Benedict's Rule*, 615.
10. Father Ignacio Ellacuría of El Salvador was murdered in 1989, along with five other Jesuits and two women employees, for their resistance to the military and their dedication to the indigenous and poor. The Jesuits were also very effective in challenging their college students to reject their lives of privilege and to work toward a truly democratic

government. The families became enraged that their children were embracing values at odds with their lifestyle as members of the ruling oligarchy invested in power and greed. I rely heavily upon the work of Doctor María Pilar Aquino of the University of San Diego in a paper she presented at Seattle University in 1999. See also Ellacuría and Sobrino, *Mysterium Liberationis*, and Ellacuría, *Conversión de la Iglesia*.

11. From a talk given by María Pilar Aquino at Seattle University in the summer of 1999.
12. Ibid.
13. Ellacuría, "Reign of God," 65.
14. Ibid., 66–67.
15. Ellacuría, "Reign of God," 64, 68.
16. Martin Luther King, Jr., *Strength to Love*, as quoted in Bass, *Practicing Our Faith*, 136.
17. Ellacuría, "Liberación," 697. The translation from Spanish into English is by Doctor María Pilar Aquino.
18. See chapter 9.
19. Aquino, *Our Cry for Life*, 82.
20. María Pilar Aquino, in her presentation at Seattle University in 1999. The expression "kingdom of hell" was used by Archbishop Oscar Romero in reference to the living reality of his people: the violence, torture, death squads, and revocation of all civil and human rights.
21. Carrier, *Culture of Modernity*, 73.

Glossary of Terms

abba—A man who is a spiritual mentor or leader, either for one or more individuals or as the head of a monastery.

accidie—An inability to be committed to the spiritual journey. It is a carelessness, listlessness, indifference, or laziness toward the hard interior work of conversion and transformation. It is a failure to appropriate Christian values.

amma—A woman who is a spiritual mentor or leader, either for one or more individuals or as the head of a monastery.

anchoress/anchorite—A solitary, residing either in a cave or a cell. In later Christianity, an anchoress/anchorite lived in a cell physically attached to a church. In Eastern Christianity, this term is used interchangeably with *amma/abba*.

apatheia—Intense purity of passion; a passion that is singularly directed toward God, not to be confused with passivity or suppression of emotions. Passion, or powerful emotions, can be a creative life force that assists and supports us on the inner journey. Evagrius Ponticus once said *desert apatheia has a daughter whose name is love.* Apatheia deepens our capacity for love and desire for God. Also known as "purity of heart."

ascetic—A person who dedicates every aspect of her/his life to contemplation and seeking union with God. An ascetic lives an austere life and has a regular practice of fasting, prayer, self-denial, and generosity toward the poor. An anchorite or hermit is one who withdraws from society in order to live alone. This solitary life is sought in order to seek God intensely and without disruptions. An anchorite or hermit is generally equivalent to a desert ascetic.

catechesis—Instruction and training in the way of Jesus Christ. It is to teach the Good News with all its commands, demands, and graces. This term particularly applies to preparing new believers for baptism and formal reception into the Catholic Church.

cell—A single room or cave, very simple, even austere, used as a place for living, work, and prayer. The cell is the place where one encounters God in solitude.

cenobite/cenobitic—The form of Christian monasticism most common today where seekers live together under a common rule and leader.

christology—The study and explanation of who Jesus of Nazareth is: as human and as the Divine Son of God. There is a large body of writing over the centuries attempting to explain how Jesus is fully human and fully God.

communion of Saints—All those seekers and believers who have gone before us as well as those alive today. It is an awareness that there are no time constraints in God's family and that through Christ we are all one, so all saints—past and present—are present with us.

compunction—Contrition or remorse. In the desert tradition, compunction is understood as a piercing of our heart by sorrow. This is considered to be healing and necessary for inner growth.

conversion—A spiritual change in priorities and commitments; a spiritual revitalization and reorientation; to live with a new heart.

deacon—From the Greek *diakonos* meaning servant or helper. This is an ordained office, related to priesthood. For the first several centuries, there was no separate designation between women and men as deacons; both genders were called deacon. Only later did gender differentiation set in (deacon for men and deaconess for women).

detachment—In desert spirituality, detachment is the process of letting go of the inner attachment to material objects, personal reputation, and position in society, attitudes, and emotions. With detachment, one can own possessions without being possessed by them. It is true simplicity.

diaspora—To be driven, as a community or ethnic group, from one's historic home, due to political, religious, or racial strife. This would be a group forced to live apart and abroad from their homeland. Native Americans and African Americans, for example, are considered *in diaspora*.

discernment—In the spiritual journey it is the daily practice of perceiving and understanding how the Holy Spirit is leading us. We then act on this discernment in choosing to follow God's Will in our life. Discernment recognizes that God is intimately interested in the quality of and direction for our life, and that we were created with passions, interests, and gifts, for particular purposes. When we are in an intimate relationship with God, we are interested in what God desires for us.

discernment of spirits—To test and discern religious influences upon a person, group, or idea. In Christian tradition, a wise person is sought to prayerfully listen and distinguish between evil and God's voice: *Is this of God? Would this commitment, course of action, possession, decision move me toward or away from God?* The language comes from an era that saw demonic influence acting in humanity.

Divine Office—Involves chanting the psalms and sections of scripture and scripture-based prayer. Most popular in use is the Morning and Evening Office. However many contemplative traditions, following the example of the ascetics, pray seven times each day. The Divine Office is another name for Liturgy of the Hours, or *Opus Dei*. These terms are all interchangeable.

enmeshment—When a person has difficulty separating emotionally from another person, therefore confusing one's own needs, issues, and emotions with the other person' needs, issues, and emotions. It implies disconnection from oneself and struggles to know oneself. Enmeshment can result in struggles with addiction and co-dependency.

eremitic—A person who lives a life of intense solitude. It also can refer to a religious tradition where solitaries live alone, but within proximity of one another, such as the Carthusian monastics today.

Eucharist—Greek, meaning *thanksgiving*. Also known as Holy Communion, the sacrament that commemorates celebrates Christ's death and resurrection. In the Gospels we read the account of the Last Supper, where Jesus identified himself with the bread that is to be broken and the cup that is to be shared, and commanded his followers to *do this in memory of me*. The assembly with the Presider petitions the Holy Spirit to transform the bread and wine with the body and blood of Christ. In sharing Eucharist together, the believing community is strengthened in unity and empowered to serve Christ. Eucharist is an expression of the living body of Christ. It is the Christian liturgical sacrament in which the Church remembers, celebrates, and proclaims Jesus' life, death, and resurrection.

Evil One—Also called Satan or the devil—the accuser, slanderer, adversary and perjurer. This is Lucifer, the fallen archangel, and the embodiment of total evil, totally other from God.

fear of God—Awe and respect for the immanence and yet *total otherness* of God. Desert Spirituality teaches that we are totally and utterly dependent upon the Divine while being drawn and attracted to a deepened relationship with God. It is not being *afraid* of God.

feminism—School of interpretation that seeks to understand ways that the voice and perspective of women have been suppressed and silenced. Religious feminism seeks to discover the ways that the experiences of women have been suppressed in sacred texts, in the interpretation of sacred texts, the ways religious traditions have imaged the Holy, and in the liturgical worship of the Holy. Religious feminism of the West has grown in recent decades with significant encounters with women from diverse cultures and the Third World.

grace—God's self-gift, freely given, that enables us to move beyond our woundedness and sin, embracing God's call and gift in our lives. Grace acknowledges the unknowing and mystery of the spiritual journey.

hermeneutics—A way of analyzing and assessing texts and events in order to better understand what happened and why, to recover lost understandings and traditions, and to discern how God is moving in our midst. It is a process applied to diverse concepts and ideas including literature, historical events, theology, and sacred Scripture. These differing kinds of analysis are ways of thinking critically. At the simplest level, each person is and has their own hermeneutic; that is, their own way of seeing and interpreting life experiences.

hermit—A person who withdraws from society in order to live alone. A solitary. See "anchorite."

heterodox—Meaning unorthodox, or not quite orthodox. In the Christological debates of the Fourth Century, the heterodox position held that Christ was either fully divine and only "appeared" human, or that he was fully human and not quite divine as the Creator is divine. This term can have important political implications. Many movements, or even churches in particular geographical locations, were called heterodox for having women and freed slaves in positions of leadership. Scholars today are reinvestigating movements long accused of heresy or heterodoxy to uncover portions of our tradition lost in political wrangling.

idolatry—Blind adoration, reverence, devotion to anything that is not God. People, things, relationships, ideas, etc. can come to so consume and possess our lives, minds, and hearts that we lose sight of God.

interior freedom—Through God's grace freely given, the seeker embraces and grows in mental, emotional. and spiritual freedom. With interior freedom, the seeker has grown in apatheia/purity of heart and is able to make and act upon discerned choices rather than being thrown about by compulsions and addictions. With interior freedom there is greater awareness of God's faithful and continued presence in the seeker's life. It is a gift and the fruit of the hard work of spiritual discipline.

laura—A naturally hewn cave that a desert dweller would adapt to become "home"; the cell where the desert solitary pursued the interior journey.

lectio divina—Reflective, meditative reading of sacred texts. The intent is prayerful formation of heart and mind rather than gaining information.

Lent—The season of the Christian Church calendar when seekers focus on transformation of heart and spirit in anticipation of the Holy Triduum: Holy Thursday, Good Friday, Holy Saturday, and Easter Sunday.

Liturgy of the Hours—See "Divine Office."

Lives—Biographies of ammas, abbas, martyrs, and saints, often commissioned by family members or religious communities. These were usually composed in a particular style with the intent of converting the reader. A factual account in our modern, scientific sense was not the primary concern.

The Master—The anonymous Roman/Italian author of the Rule of the Master, the monastic document that heavily influenced Benedict's writings.

monastery—People gathered around a spiritual leader, sharing a common life and prayer. There is usually a degree of seclusion from the general public as well as some form of religious vows.

monastic promise—In making a lifelong commitment to the monastic way of life as a vowed religious, the monk/nun professes the monastic promise at the altar of the monastery chapel and before the prioress or abbot and the monastic community. The monastic promise includes stability, obedience, and fidelity to the monastic way of life (Latin: *conversatio morum*). Chaste celibacy and simplicity are assumed within the context of monastic profession. Monastic profession intensifies baptismal commitment.

monk—From the Greek *monos*, meaning "one" or "solitary." A person —man or woman—who lives in a monastery.

mutual obedience—An important concept throughout Benedict's writings where the Gospel and the Rule are the common guidelines that all members of the monastery live under. With mutual obedience, hierarchy is rendered ineffective: the prioress or abbot; the most-senior members along with the newest members; the nobility and low-caste; the best educated and the illiterate members of the community all seek to obey one another, while serving shoulder-to-shoulder under the Gospel and the Rule.

oblate—A person who has made a commitment to a particular Benedictine monastery, promising to live the Benedictine way of life within the context of lay life commitments and ministry. A lay Benedictine.

oblation—The term used when oblates make their monastic profession. Oblation is made to a particular monastery, but oblates can transfer their oblation to another monastery if needed.

Opus Dei—Latin for "work of God." For Benedict, the Opus Dei was prayer and especially the Liturgy of the Hours or Divine Office. Prayer was to be given precedence over everything else.

oratory—A small chapel, not a parish church, dedicated exclusively to prayer. In monasticism, the oratory is usually the monastery chapel.

ordo—The ordo is a kind of schedule for the liturgical year, giving dates for celebrating universally recognized holy days (such as Christmas, Easter, and Pentecost) as well as local feasts and saints. Each region or religious order may have their own ordo: Franciscans might favor Franciscan saints, Benedictines remember the monastics who have died (this can include members of the monastery that have gone before us), etc. Each monastery either develops its own ordo or adopts another monastery's ordo.

orthodox—Meaning the correct religious doctrine. In the Christological debates, this position held that Christ was fully human *and* fully divine. This was the emerging position of prominent theologians and bishops that resulted in the Nicene Creed and Trinitarian theology.

patriarchal systems—Are hierarchical, meaning a power structure from the lowest strata of society (and therefore including the largest number of people) with the least amount of power toward the elite strata of society (and therefore including the least number of people). The elite are men and they rule.

People of God—In the broadest and most inclusive sense, all people who seek and serve God within their respective religious traditions. For Christians, the People of God are all who respond to God's unconditional love and the baptismal call to be the Good News of Jesus to all.

purity of heart—See "apatheia."

repentance—From the Greek word, *metanoia*: *meta* meaning with and *noieo* meaning understanding. Related to the Greek *metanoeo*: to change one's mind or feelings. Repentance is a deep inner change in disposition and attitude; a movement from despair, regret, and remorse toward serenity.

resurrection—The Christian belief that God overcame death by raising Jesus from the dead after he was crucified. As followers of Christ, we believe that we too will be raised from the dead—as death no longer has power over us. In spirituality, mystics and wise teachers also speak of the little deaths and resurrections in our daily life that God helps us with.

Rule of Benedict—This spiritual document outlines a way of life for those interested in the monastic life. It was written toward the end of Benedict of Nursia's life.

rule—The code that regulates the common life of a community. Although these can be legal in nature, most rules, especially in their earliest forms, are spiritual documents. Rules define prayer, commitment, simplicity and good works. Rules also exhort community members in their pursuit of holiness and lay the foundation for the direction and vision of the community's existence.

Sanhedrin—The ruling body of the Jewish community in Jerusalem and environs; some were supporters of Jesus and some were his detractors.

Sayings—The oral teachings of an amma/abba to their followers that are remembered, passed on, and eventually written down.

Seder—The ceremonial meal held during Passover commemorating the deliverance of the Jewish people from Egyptian captivity—the Exodus. Seder is celebrated in the home, and is presided over by the female head of the family, usually the mother.

Senpectae—The Senpectae are the wise elders of the monastery: not necessarily the oldest members, but those who have gained hard won wisdom regarding the monastic life.

spiritual direction—Also called spiritual companioning, it is a relationship where the presence, actions, callings, and directions of God are sought, and discerned. The "spiritual director" is a seeker trained in the ability to listen to the seeker and the movements of the Holy Spirit. The director asks evocative questions, reflects back what is heard, and affirms the seeker's growing God-awareness. This ancient tradition, for Christians, began in the desert.

spirituality—A former professor of mine, Phil Boroughs, S.J., defines Christian spirituality as "the experience and the expression of the revelation of God in the Spirit of Jesus, to which the believer lovingly responds in prayer and service as an individual, as a participant in a faith community, and as a member of the human family within creation."

statio—The practice of gathering in some kind of formation (usually two lines) outside the monastery chapel in silent and prayerful reflection in preparation for the Liturgy of the Hours. Usually the monastics, upon a given signal, enter in slow and dignified procession, make a gesture toward the altar and other monastics before proceeding to their choir stalls.

tradition—Transmission of beliefs, doctrines, teachings, rituals, and historical patterns of interpretation of sacred texts. For monastics, this includes rituals and sacred texts that shape and support the monastic tradition; the Church Fathers and Mothers; monastic authors; and various monastic texts and rules.

Triduum—The Christian days of Holy Thursday, Good Friday, and Holy Saturday, which commemorate Jesus' crucifixion, death, and entombment.

Vulgate—A translation of the Bible from the Hebrew and Greek into the vernacular (thus "vulgar") Latin, which was the common language of the people of the Roman Empire.

Selected Bibliography

Our beliefs, values and ways of thinking are influenced by so many sources: life experiences, people, and the written word. Besides the sources I directly quote, I have included sources that influenced my own thinking and may enrich your inner journey as well.

Aquino, María Pilar. *Our Cry for Life: Feminist Theology from Latin America*. Maryknoll, NY: Orbis Books, 1993.

Arnold, Johann Christoph. *Seeking Peace: Notes and Conversations Along the Way*. Farmington, PA: Plough, 1998.

Bass, Dorothy C., ed. *Practicing Our Faith: A Way of Life for a Searching People*. San Francisco: Jossey-Bass Publishers, 1997.

Belisle, Peter-Damian. *The Language of Silence: The Changing Face of Monastic Solitude*. Maryknoll, NY: Orbis Books, 2003.

Böckmann, Aquinata, O.S.B. "Benedictine Mysticism: Dynamic Spirituality in RB." *Tjurunga* 57 (1999): 85–101.

———. "Benedictine Prayer Tradition and the Jesus Prayer." *Benedictines* 63:2 (1989): 18–29.

———. "Le Chiasme dans la Règle Bènédictine." *Revue Bènédictine* 95 (1985): 25–38.

———. "Christ in the Rule of St. Benedict." *Monastic Studies* 10 (1974): 19–128.

———. "The Experience of God in the Rule of St. Benedict." *Benedictines* 51:2 (1998): 6–19.

———. "On the Oratory of the Monastery." *The American Benedictine Review* 49 (1998): 60–85.

———. *Perspektiven der Regula Benedicti*. Münsterschwarzach, Germany: Vier Türme-Verlag, 1986.

———. "RB 5: Benedict's Chapter on Obedience." *The American Benedictine Review* 45:2 (June 1994): 109–130.

———. "Seeking God: The Benedictine Way." *Tjurunga* 53 (1997): 5–22.

————. "Wenn einem Bruder Unmögliches aufgetragenwird." *Erbe und Auftrag* (1992).

Bongie, Elizabeth Bryson, trans. *The Life and Regimen of the Blessed and Holy Teacher Syncletica*. Toronto, ON: Peregrina Press, 1995.

Bons-Storm, Riet. *The Incredible Woman: Listening to Women's Silences in Pastoral Care and Counseling*. Nashville, TN: Abingdon Press, 1996.

Brock, Rita Nakashima. *Journeys by Heart: A Christology of Erotic Power*. New York: Crossroad Publishing, 1988.

Brueggemann, Walter. *Praying the Psalms*. Winona, MN: St. Mary's Press, 1986.

Canham, Elizabeth J. *Heart Whispers: Benedictine Wisdom for Today*. Nashville, TN: Upper Room Books, 1999.

Carr, Anne E. *Transforming Grace: Christian Tradition and Women's Experience*. New York: Continuum, 1996.

Carrier, Herve, S.J. *Evangelizing the Culture of Modernity*. Maryknoll, NY: Orbis Books, 1993.

Carruth, Shawn, O.S.B. "The Monastic Virtue of Obedience, Silence and Humility: a Feminist Perspective." *The American Benedictine Review* 51:2 (June 2000): 121–147.

————. "Turning the Day into Night: Reflections on the Hours." *Tjurunga* 55 (1998): 5–18.

Carruthers, Mary. *The Craft of Thought: Meditation, Rhetoric, and the Making of Images, 400–1200*. Cambridge: Cambridge University Press, 1998.

Casey, Michael, O.C.S.O. "From the Silence of God to the God of Silence: The Experience of Progress in *Lectio Divina*." *Tjurunga* (1992): 3–25.

————. *A Guide to Living in the Truth: Saint Benedict's Teaching on Humility*. Liguori, MO: Liguori/Triumph, 2001.

Chittister, Joan, O.S.B. *Heart of Flesh: A Feminist Spirituality for Women and Men*. Grand Rapids, MI: Eerdmans Publishing, 1998.

Clarkson, Benedict. "The Rule of Benedict and the Concept of Self-Actualization." *Cistercian Studies Quarterly* 10 (1975): 22–45.

Conference of American Benedictine Prioresses. *Discerning Community Leadership: The Benedictine Tradition*. Ferdinand, IN: Monastery Immaculate Conception, 1993.

————. *Upon This Tradition: Five Statements on Monastic Values in the Lives of American Benedictine Sisters*. Reprinted with Prologues and Updates. Privately Printed by the Conference of American Benedictine Prioresses, 2001.

Conn, Joann Welski, ed. *Women's Spirituality: Resources for Christian Development*. Mahwah, NJ: Paulist Press, 1996.

Conn, Walter E. *The Desiring Self: Rooting Pastoral Counseling and Spiritual Direction in Self-Transcendence*. Mahwah, NJ: Paulist Press, 1998.

Copeland, Shawn. "Racism and the Vocation of the Christian Theologian." *Spiritus: A Journal of Christian Spirituality* 2:1 (Spring 2002): 15–29.

Craghan, John. *The Psalms: Prayers for the Ups, Downs, and In-Betweens of Life*. Wilmington, DE: Michael Glazier, 1985.

Dennis, Marie, Renny Golden, and Scott Wright. *Oscar Romero: Reflections on His Life and Writings*. Maryknoll, NY: Orbis Books, 2000.

Deutsch, Celia M. *Lady Wisdom, Jesus, and the Sages: Metaphor and Social Context in Matthew's Gospel*. Valley Forge, PA: Trinity Press International, 1996.

de Dreuille, Mayeul, O.S.B. *The Rule of Saint Benedict: A Commentary in Light of World Ascetic Traditions*. Mahwah, NJ: The Newman Press, 2002.

Dumont, Charles. "A Phenomenological Approach to Humility: Chapter VII of the Rule of Saint Benedict." *Cistercian Studies Quarterly* 45 (1985): 283–302.

Dunn, Marilyn. *The Emergence of Monasticism: From the Desert Fathers to the Early Middle Ages*. Oxford: Blackwell Publishers, 2000.

Eberle, Luke, O.S.B., trans. *Rule of the Master: Regula Magistri*. Kalamazoo, MI: Cistercian Publications, 1977.

Ellacuría, Ignacio, S.J. "Liberacion," in *Conceptos Fundamentales del Cristianismo*. Edited by Casiano Floristan and Juan Jose Tamayo. Madrid: Trotta, 1993.

————. *Conversión de la Iglesia al Reino de Dios, Para Anunciarlo y Realizarlo en la Historia*. Santander, Spain: Sal Terrae, 1984.

————. "Persecution for the Sake of the Reign of God," in *Companions of Jesus: The Jesuit Martyrs of El Salvador*. Edited by Jon Sobrino, S.J. Maryknoll, NY: Orbis Books, 1990.

Ellacuría, Ignacio, S.J., and Jon Sobrino S.J., eds. *Mysterium Liberationis: Fundamental Concepts in Liberation Theology*. Maryknoll, NY: Orbis Books, 1993.

Elm, Susanna. *"Virgins of God": The Making of Asceticism in Late Antiquity*. Oxford: Clarendon Press, 1994.

Fehribach, Adeline. *The Women in the Life of the Bridegroom: A Feminist Historical-Literary Analysis of the Female Characters in the Fourth Gospel*. Collegeville, MN: Michael Glazier, 1998.

Feiss, Hugh, O.S.B. *Essential Monastic Wisdom: Writings on the Contemplative Life*. New York: Harper San Francisco, 1999.

Fischer, Kathleen. *Transforming Fire: Women Using Anger Creatively*. Mahwah, NJ: Paulist Press, 1999.

————. *Women at the Well: Feminist Perspectives on Spiritual Direction*. Mahwah, NJ: Paulist Press, 1988.

Forman, Mary, O.S.B. "Scriptural Exegesis in the Rule of Benedict." Ph.D. diss. Centre for Medieval Studies, University of Toronto, 1994.

Fredriksen, Paula. *Jesus of Nazareth, King of the Jews: A Jewish Life and the Emergence of Christianity*. New York: Knopf, 1999.

Frigge, Marielle, O.S.B. "Reflections of a Monastic Feminist." *The American Benedictine Review* 50:2 (1999): 121–148.

Fry, Timothy, Timothy Horner, and Imogene Baker, eds. *RB 1980: The Rule of St. Benedict in Latin and English With Notes*. Collegeville, MN: The Liturgical Press, 1981.

Gebara, Ivone. *Out of the Depths: Women's Experience of Evil and Salvation*. Minneapolis, MN: Fortress Press, 2002.

Gilligan, Carol. *In a Different Voice: Psychological Theory and Women's Development*. Cambridge, MA: Harvard University Press, 1982.

Gilson, Anne Bathurst. *Eros Breaking Free: Interpreting Sexual Theo-Ethics*. Cleveland, OH: Pilgrim Press, 1995.

Glaz, Maxine, and Jeanne Stevenson Moessner, eds. *Women in Travail and Transition: A New Pastoral Care*. Minneapolis, MN: Fortress, 1991.

Graff, Ann O'Hara, ed. *In the Embrace of God: Feminist Approaches to Theological Anthropology*. Maryknoll, NY: Orbis Books, 1995.

Gregory the Great. *The Life of Saint Benedict*, with commentary by Adalbert de Vogüé, O.S.B., Hilary Costello, and Eoin de Bhaldraithe trans. Petersham, MA: St. Bede's Publications, 1993.

Guevin, Benedict, O.S.B. "Authenticity: Is This the Meaning of Benedictine Spirituality? A Response to Antoine Vergote." *The American Benedictine Review* 47:3 (September 1996): 225–239.

Harrington, Christina. *Women in a Celtic Church: Ireland 450–1150*. Cambridge, MA: Oxford University Press, 2001.

Herman, Judith, M.D. *Trauma and Recovery: The Aftermath of Violence— From Domestic Abuse to Political Terror*. New York: Basic Books, 1992.

Heyward, Carter. *Touching Our Strength: The Erotic as Power and the Love of God*. San Francisco: Harper and Row, 1989.

Hildebrand, Stephen M. "Oboedientia and Oboedire in the Rule of St. Benedict: A Study of Their Theological and Monastic Meanings." *The American Benedictine Review* 52:4 (December 2001): 421–436.

Horst, Elisabeth A. *Recovering the Lost Self: Shame-Healing for Victims of Clergy Sexual Abuse*. Collegeville, MN: The Liturgical Press, 1998.

Huerre, Denis, O.S.B., "Monastic Hospitality and the Conversion of the Monk." *The American Benedictine Review* 44:3 (1993).

Hume, Cardinal Basil, O.S.B. *The Mystery of the Cross*. London: Darton, Longman and Todd, 1998.

Johnson, Elizabeth, C.S.J. *She Who Is: The Mystery of God in Feminist Theological Discourse*. New York: Crossroad Publishing, 1992.

———. *Friends of God and Prophets: A Feminist Theological Reading of the Communion of Saints*. New York: Continuum, 1998.

Jordan, Judith V., Alexandra G. Kaplan, Jean Baker Miller, Irene P. Stiver, and Janet L. Surrey. *Women's Growth in Connection: Writings from the Stone Center*. New York: The Guilford Press, 1991.

Kardong, Terrence, O.S.B. *Benedict's Rule: A Translation and Commentary*. Collegeville, MN: The Liturgical Press, 1996.

———. "Benedict's Use of Cassianic Formulae for Spiritual Progress." *Studia Monastica* 34 (1992): 233–252.

———. "The Biblical Roots of Benedict's Teaching on the Fear of the Lord." *Tjurunga* 43 (1992): 25–50.

———. "Clarifications of Benedict's Chapter on Humility: A Reply to Francis Seeburger's Article 'Humility, Maturity and the Fear of God.'" *The American Benedictine Review* 50:1 (March, 1999): 12–29.

———. "Coming Late: Benedict's Prohibition Against Tardiness in RB 43." *Regulae Benedicti Studia* 18 (1995): 115–128.

———. "Hard Obedience: Benedict's Chapter 68 and Beyond." *Regulae Benedicti Studia* 13 (1986): 193–202.

———. "The Heights of Humility." *Studia Monastica* 38 (1996): 263–269.

———. "Justitia in the Rule of Benedict." *Studia Monastica* 24 (1982): 43–73.

———. "Respect for Persons in the Holy Rule: Benedict's Contribution to Human Rights." *Cistercian Studies* 27 (1992): 200–207.

———. "To Receive All as Christ." *Cistercian Studies* 19 (1984): 195–207.

Kegan, Robert. *The Evolving Self: Problem and Process in Human Development.* Cambridge, MA: Harvard University Press, 1982.

Kegan, Robert, and Lisa Laskow Lahey. *How the Way We Talk Can Change the Way We Work: Seven Languages for Transformation.* San Francisco: Jossey-Bass Publishers, 2000.

Killen, Patricia O'Connell. *Finding Our Voices: Women, Wisdom, and Faith.* New York: Crossroad Publishing, 1997.

Krawiec, Rebecca. *Shenoute and the Women of the White Monastery: Egyptian Monasticism in Late Antiquity.* New York: Oxford University Press, 2002.

LaCugna, Catherine Mowry, ed. *Freeing Theology: The Essentials of Theology in Feminist Perspective.* San Francisco: HarperSanFrancisco, 1993.

Luckman, Harriet, and Linda Kulzer, eds. *Purity of Heart in Early Ascetic and Monastic Literature.* Collegeville, MN: The Liturgical Press, 1999.

McClure, John, and Nancy Ramsay, eds. *Telling the Truth: Preaching About Sexual and Domestic Violence.* Cleveland, OH: Pilgrim Press, 1998.

McGuire, Meredith. "Why Bodies Matter: A Sociological Reflection on Spirituality and Materiality." *Spiritus: A Journal of Christian Spirituality* 3:1 (Spring 2003): 1–18.

McKenna, Megan. *Prophets: Words of Fire*. Maryknoll, NY: Orbis Books, 2001.

McNamara, Jo Ann. *Sisters in Arms: Catholic Nuns through Two Millennia*. Cambridge, MA: Harvard University Press, 1996.

Macy, Gary. *The Banquet's Wisdom: A Short History of the Theologies of the Lord's Supper*. Mahwah, NJ: Paulist Press, 1992.

———. *Treasures from the Storeroom: Medieval Religion and the Eucharist*. Collegeville, MN: The Liturgical Press, 1999.

Mayer, Suzanne, I.H.M. *Celebrating the Woman You Are*. Mahwah, NJ: Paulist Press, 1995.

Milhaven, Annie Lally, ed. *Sermons Seldom Heard: Women Proclaim Their Lives*. New York: Crossroad Publishing, 1991.

Moessner, Jeanne Stevenson, ed. *In Her Own Time: Women and Developmental Issues in Pastoral Care*. Minneapolis, MN: Fortress Press, 2000.

———. *Through the Eyes of Women: Insights for Pastoral Care*. Minneapolis, MN: Fortress Press, 1996.

Monastic Profession: Commitment to a Way of Life. A Study Guide Prepared by the InterFederation/Congregation Committee on Monastic Profession, 2000.

Monks of New Skete. *In the Spirit of Happiness: Spiritual Wisdom for Living*. Boston, MA: Little, Brown, 1999.

Nowell, Irene, O.S.B. "The Psalms: Living Water for Our Lives." *Benedictines* 52:1 (Summer 1999): 22–33.

Nugent, Andrew, O.S.B. "Benedict: A Sense of Prayer." *The American Benedictine Review* 50:2 (June 1999): 149–160.

Pennington, Basil, O.C.S.O. *Rule and Life: An Interdisciplinary Symposium*. Spencer, MA: Cistercian Publications, 1971.

Peterson, Marilyn R. *At Personal Risk: Boundary Violations in Professional-Client Relationships*. New York: W.W. Norton and Co. 1992.

Pieris, Aloysius, S.J. "Ecumenism in the Churches and the Unfinished Agenda of the Holy Spirit." *Spiritus: A Journal of Christian Spirituality* 3:1 (Spring 2003): 53–67.

Pfatteicher, Philip H. *Liturgical Spirituality*. Valley Forge, PA: Trinity Press International, 1997.

Peifer, Claude J., O.S.B. *Monastic Spirituality*. New York: Sheed and Ward, 1966.

Raasch, Juana, O.S.B. "The Monastic Concept of Purity of Heart and Its Sources." *Studia Monastica* 8 (1966): 7–33, 183–213; 10 (1968): 7–555; 11 (1969): 269–314; 12 (1970): 7–41.

Ramsey, Boniface, O.P., trans. and commentary. *John Cassian: The Conferences*. Ancient Christian Writers 57. Mahwah, NJ: Paulist, 1997.

———. *John Cassian: The Institutes*. Ancient Christian Writers 58. Mahwah, NJ: Paulist Press, 2000.

Rappaport, Roy A. *Ritual and Religion in the Making of Humanity*. Cambridge Studies in Social and Cultural Anthropology. New York: Cambridge University Press, 1999.

Robinson, David. *The Family Cloister: Benedictine Wisdom for the Home*. New York: Crossroad Publishing, 2000.

Romero, Oscar. *The Violence of Love*. Farmington, PA: Plough Publishing, 1998.

Saussy, Carroll. *God Images and Self Esteem: Empowering Women in a Patriarchal Society*. Louisville, KY: Westminster John Knox Press, 1991.

———. *The Gift of Anger: A Call to Faithful Action*. Louisville, KY: Westminster John Knox Press, 1995.

Schneiders, Sandra, I.H.M. *The Revelatory Text: Interpreting the New Testament as Sacred Scripture*. New York: HarperCollins, 1991.

———. *Finding the Treasure: Locating Catholic Religious Life in a New Ecclesial and Cultural Context*. Mahwah, NJ: Paulist Press, 2000.

———. *Selling All: Commitment, Consecrated Celibacy, and Community in Catholic Religious Life*. Mahwah, NJ: Paulist Press, 2001.

Seeburger, Francis F. "Humility, Maturity, and the Fear of God: Reflections on RB 7." *The American Benedictine Review* 46:2 (June 1995): 149–168.

Shannon, William. *Silence on Fire: The Prayer of Awareness*. New York: Crossroad Publishing, 1991.

———. *Thomas Merton's Paradise Journey: Writings on Contemplation*. Cincinnati, OH: St. Anthony Messenger Press, 2000.

Smith, Susan, Obl. O.S.B. "Co-creating the Household of God: Two Models of Hospitality." *Benedictines* (Winter 1993): 41–42.

Sobrino, Jon, S.J. *Archbishop Romero: Memories and Reflections*. Translated by Robert R. Barr. Maryknoll, NY: Orbis Books, 1990.

———. "Monseñor Romero, a Salvadoran and a Christian." *Spiritus: A Journal of Christian Spirituality* 1:2 (Fall 2001): 143–155.

———. *Witnesses to the Kingdom: The Martyrs of El Salvador and the Crucified Peoples*. Maryknoll, NY: Orbis Books, 1990.

Sobrino, Jon, S.J., Ignacio Ellacuría, et al. *Companions of Jesus: The Jesuit Martyrs of El Salvador*. Maryknoll, NY: Orbis Books, 1990.

Stasiak, Kurt, O.S.B. "Four Kinds of Monks: Four Obstacles to Seeking God." *The American Benedictine Review* 45:2 (September 1994): 303–320.

Stewart, Columba, O.S.B. *Prayer and Community: The Benedictine Tradition*. Maryknoll, NY: Orbis, 1998.

———. "'We'? Reflections on Affinity and Dissonance in Reading Early Monastic Literature." *Spiritus: A Journal of Christian Spirituality* 1:1 (Spring 2001): 93–102.

Swan, Laura, O.S.B. *The Forgotten Desert Mothers: Sayings, Lives, and Stories of Early Christian Women*. Mahwah, NJ: Paulist Press, 2001.

———. "Hospitality and the Prophetic." *Pre-Conference Proceedings of the American Benedictine Academy Convention Papers*, August 1998.

Tamez, Elsa. "The Challenge to Live as Resurrected: Reflections on Romans Six and Eight." *Spiritus: A Journal of Christian Spirituality* 3:1 (Spring 2003): 86–95.

Taylor, Barbara Erakko. *Silence: Making the Journey to Inner Quiet*. Philadelphia, PA: Innisfree Press, 1997.

Vergote, Antoine. "A Psychological Approach to Humility in the Rule of Saint Benedict." *The American Benedictine Review* 39 (1988): 404–429.

de Vogüé, Adalbert, O.S.B. *Community and Abbot in the Rule of Benedict*. Kalamazoo, MI: Cistercian Publications, 1979.

_____. *The Rule of Benedict: A Doctrinal and Spiritual Commentary*. Kalamazoo, MI: Cistercian Publications, 1983.

_____. *Reading Saint Benedict: Reflections on the Rule*. Kalamazoo, MI: Cistercian Publications, 1994.

_____. "The Search for God in Saint Benedict's Rule." *Cistercian Studies Quarterly* 36:4 (2001): 437–445.

Wathen, Ambrose, O.S.B. *Silence: The Meaning of Silence in the Rule of St. Benedict*. Washington, D.C.: Cistercian Publications, 1973.

_____. "The Word of Silence: On Silence and Speech in RB." *Cistercian Studies Quarterly* 17 (1982): 195–211.

Wheatley, Margaret, and Myron Kellner-Rogers. *A Simpler Way*. San Francisco: Berrett-Koehler, 1996.

Wink, Walter. *Engaging the Powers: Discernment and Resistance in a World of Domination*. Minneapolis, MN: Fortress Press, 1992.

Wolter, Maurus, O.S.B. *The Principles of Monasticism*. Translated, edited, and annotated by Bernard A. Sause, O.S.B. St. Louis: B. Herder Book Co., 1962.

Laura Swan, O.S.B., is prioress of Saint Placid Priory, a Benedictine monastery in the Pacific Northwest. Swan holds graduate degrees in theology and spirituality. She is the author of *The Forgotten Desert Mothers* (Paulist Press) and *History of North American Benedictine Women* (Writers Club Press).